Old Salem
The Official Guidebook

Restored buildings and heirloom gardens create the ambience of the Moravian town of Salem between 1766 and 1856.

Old Salem

The Official Guidebook

Text by
Penelope Niven

Architecture Keys and Street Guide by
Cornelia B. Wright

Old Salem Inc. Winston-Salem, North Carolina

Welcome to Old Salem!

In Old Salem you can walk timeworn pathways, explore historic buildings, and admire decorative arts, crafts, and toys. You can hear ancient liturgy and old hymns, partake of Moravian traditions, taste bread and cookies made from old receipts, and stroll in the hush of God's Acre. You can learn how Old Salem was conceived and created, how it grew and changed.

Perhaps your curiosity about the people of the past brings you here in hopes that history will shed light on the present and the future. Perhaps you seek to understand the spirit of the Moravians, or wonder about daily life in their idealistic society.

In this unique place, you will find compelling stories of the people who lived in the town of Salem and the outlying villages of the Wachovia Settlement. You will learn about the devout Moravians whose personal stories are interwoven with the history of a religion as well as the history of a congregation town, of Piedmont North Carolina, and of the United States. And history often begins with a traveler on an untraveled road. . .

After a grueling climb on foot and horseback "over terrible mountains, and often through very dangerous ways," Bishop August Gottlieb Spangenberg and his traveling companions set up a rough camp in the Carolina wilderness on November 29, 1752. "We are here in a region that has perhaps been seldom visited since the creation of the world," Spangenberg wrote in his diary. "We are some 70 or 80 miles from the last settlement in North Carolina. . . But, thank God, we are all well, cheerful, and content, and thankful to our Heavenly Father. . . ."

Spangenberg and his companions were Moravians, members of Unitas Fratrum, or the Unity of Brethren, as their church had long been known in Europe. The church was nearly three centuries old when John, Lord Carteret, Earl Granville offered the Moravians0 the opportunity to buy a hundred thousand acres of his land holdings in the Carolina colony. Lord Granville was impressed with the success of the Moravian settlement in Bethlehem, Pennsylvania, as were many others.

In London, Parliament passed an act in 1749 to encourage the Moravians to "settle in His Majesty's Colonies in America," promising that Moravian settlers would "be indulged with a full Liberty of Conscience, and in the Exercise of the Religion they profess. . . ."

August Spangenberg, then the Moravian Vicar General of America, was put in charge of choosing the land for the Carolina settlement. He was 48 years old when he made the treacherous, exhausting trip from Pennsylvania to Edenton, North Carolina, and then to the far reaches of the Carolina frontier. Born in Germany, Spangenberg had already served as a university professor in Europe and a pioneer in America. He led the first Moravian colonists to Georgia in 1735, and was a force in establishing the Moravians in Pennsylvania.

Spangenberg was as much at home on horseback in Indian country in the American colonies as he was serving on the central boards of the Moravian church in Europe. He was a man who could lead a worship service; track buffalo; tramp unexplored woodland with a surveyor; plan a vast settlement; negotiate complex financial arrangements; write a lengthy diary and several books; and mediate religious and secular disputes. His versatility, vigor and vision made Spangenberg not only the ideal Moravian but the ideal citizen in eighteenth century colonial America.

The Moravians who built Salem transplanted a staunch religious faith and a sturdy secular idealism to the rugged Carolina Backcountry. They had a threefold mission: to serve their neighbors in surrounding settlements within eighty miles of Wachovia, as they named their land; "to establish a town where the Moravian ideals of Christian living might be practically realized;" and to preach the gospel to the Indians. Out of their commitment to "common labor for the common good," the Moravians subdued the wilderness, built houses, farmed the land, established a vibrant trading center, and, for the most part, lived amicably with their neighbors.

From the earliest days the Moravians were a multicultural society. The first colonists dispatched to North Carolina in 1753 were born in Germany, Norway, Danish Holstein, Pennsylvania, or New York. In 1766, the Moravians in Wachovia welcomed "the first company of Brethren and Sisters coming to us direct from Europe by way of Charlestown [South Carolina]. . . ."

Enslaved Africans and African Americans lived and labored in Salem, helping to build and sustain the community. Some became members of the Moravian congregation. Because German was the primary language in the Wachovia settlement, it became the center of the "largest German-speaking black population known in the early South." Africans and African Americans in Salem frequently taught white residents to speak English, sometimes lived in dormitories with whites, and often worked shoulder to shoulder with white brethren in farm fields, mills, craft shops and homes.

The people of Salem were tangibly connected to the world at large. Many decisions about daily life, spiritual and secular, were made in the Moravian councils in Europe. Letters and travelers made their slow way from Salem to the coast, across the Atlantic Ocean to England or Germany, and back again. Moravians in Salem were tethered to Bethlehem and other Moravian communities in Pennsylvania by letters, documents, and travel.

The Carolina Moravians were more cosmopolitan than most of their Backcountry neighbors—better educated; more cultured, with their appreciation for science, music, literature, art, and fine crafts and decorative arts; better equipped for daily challenges of life, from the practice of medicine to the self-sufficiency provided by the skilled Salem work force. The town grew to be a robust commercial center, trading far and wide with colonists in the Carolinas, Virginia, and Georgia. The Moravians were conscientious citizens, shrewdly participating in colonial and then state legislative as well as commercial affairs. They also dispatched missionaries to the Cherokees and other Native Americans and supported international missions, receiving reports on mission fields around the world—from the West Indies to Greenland to Cairo.

From the Revolutionary War to the Industrial Revolution and the Civil War, external forces inevitably touched and even altered daily life in Salem. As time and events demanded, the Moravians reshaped their society, their culture, their commerce, and certain religious rules and practices.

They lived then with questions that face us now. They wrestled with the rhetoric of liberty and human rights, and the challenges of ever-increasing religious and ethnic diversity. Like citizens across the country, the people of Salem grappled with pivotal issues: the sometimes bloody quest for freedom; the tensions between a local society and an emerging nation; the national and personal wounds and scars of slavery; the upheaval of change brought on by the expansion of industrialism and capitalism; the dramatic repercussions of war; and the need to live harmoniously in Salem and the world beyond.

In February 1866, the Moravians marked their Jubilee with three days of church services and a procession of 1500 people to the cemetery, God's Acre, where the graves of the first settlers were covered with evergreen crosses. Despite their worries about the postwar economy and a "severance of family ties," they celebrated this "solemn and festive occasion" with gratitude. For a century the Moravians had simultaneously maintained their unique identity and mirrored the struggles and aspirations of their neighbors in Piedmont North Carolina, the South, and the nation.

The codes below are used in the guidebook and on the accompanying map to indicate services and amenities in Old Salem.

Dining

Overnight accomodations

Information and ticket purchase

Parking

Restrooms

Shopping

Ticket is required

Vending machines

Contents

6

1. *The History and Faith of the Moravians*

You are visiting a unique place, a congregation town that was planned, built, owned, and operated by the Moravian Church. The German-speaking men, women, and children who first lived here were hardworking pioneers who transplanted themselves and their deep religious faith from Europe to the Carolina wilderness. They were recognized as "a sober, quiet, and industrious People" whose historic church was respected in Moravia, Bohemia, Prussia, Poland, Silesia, Lusatia, and England.

As you walk the pathways these Moravians created, visit the houses and shops they built, and hear their names and their stories, this brief introduction will help you understand their history, their religious faith, and their community.

The Moravian brothers who made the treacherous journey to the backwoods of North Carolina were pilgrims, just as surely as their better-known counterparts in New England. They were, in fact, the latest in a long and venerable line of pioneers in the Moravian Church.

The Moravians had actually called themselves the Unity of the Brethren, or *Unitas Fratrum*. In the sixteenth century, the church was widely known as the Bohemian Brethren, but when English Christians began calling them Moravians in the 1730s, the name took hold in the English-speaking world. The religious movement had its center in Bohemia and Moravia, neighboring provinces in what would later become part of the country of Czechoslovakia, now the Czech Republic.

The Kralice Bible, printed in Czech. It was the first Bible translated into a modern European language (Gutenberg's Bible was in Latin). This copy was printed in 1597.

The ancient Unitas Fratrum was born in the tumultuous wake of the death of John Huss, the Catholic priest from Bohemia who challenged the authority and ethics of the established church and was burned at the stake for heresy in 1415. His surviving followers, called the Hussites, suffered terrible persecution as they defended their faith and the memory of their martyred leader. Bohemian King Wenceslas IV, by royal edict and in collusion with the Catholic Church, closed the Hussite churches in 1419. After fourteen years of Hussite Wars, the Hussite congregations existed only in scattered fragments worshipping in secret.

One small group found refuge in the barony of Lititz in Bohemia. In 1457, these pilgrims established a society, built on the principles of the New Testament, that emulated the life of the Apostles. Ten years later they established a separate church. They called themselves at first "The Brethren of the Law of Christ," and then the Unity of the Brethren. The foundation of this society marks the formal beginning of the Moravian Church, or the Unitas Fratrum.

As soon as word of their heresy reached Rome, the Brethren were declared "shameless vagabonds" and outlaws and were persecuted accordingly. Their history played out in blood and fire, in dogged footsteps through the wildernesses, in words carefully expressed in strange languages and inscribed on pages that others tried to burn, in passive resistance and active proselytizing, in pride in work, in spiritual struggle, and in stubborn faith in God and each other.

They were a half century ahead of Martin Luther's Reformation movement. By the time that Luther nailed his ninety-five theses to the Wittenberg church door in 1517, there were scattered throughout Moravia, Bohemia, and Poland four hundred Moravian congregations, with 150,000 to 200,000 members. By 1501 the Moravians had published the first Protestant hymnal. In 1593, they issued the Kralice Bible, a translation into Czech that was fourteen years in the making. It was the first complete version of the Bible to be published in a vernacular language and is still read today by Czech-speaking people. (In 1453, Gutenberg had been the first to print the Bible in any language. The King James translation of the Bible was completed in 1611.)

Early in the seventeenth century, thousands of the Brethren left Bohemia in a mass exodus to escape religious persecution, including imprisonment, torture, and even death. Their schools and churches were destroyed and their Bibles, catechisms, hymnals, and church records were burned by religious and civil authorities. The surviving congregations of the Unitas Fratrum were forced underground by the Counter-Reformation and the prolonged struggle of the Thirty Years' War, which ended in 1648. In the end, only remnants of the old congregations survived, worshipping in secret. Even in severely reduced numbers, however, the Brethren were indomitable.

Their most zealous leader during this time was John Amos Comenius (1592–1672), an extraordinary teacher and visionary who, like so many others, was forced to flee Bohemia to live in exile in Poland. He was named a bishop in 1632. Comenius called his fellow believers the "hidden seed" because they carried out their faith in secret, passing it on from one generation to the next. He believed that one day this seed would find fertile ground, blossom, and bear fruit.

As he and other refugees struggled over a snow-covered pass through the mountains of Bohemia, he prayed that God would protect the Unitas Fratrum. For the rest of his life, he made it his mission to help the Brethren preserve the "hidden seed." Comenius stressed the importance of education for all children as the key to ensuring that the ideals of the faith could survive in the hearts and minds of believers. He died in exile in Amsterdam in 1672.

John Huss

Born sometime between 1369 and 1372 to a poor Bohemian family, John Huss was ordained a Catholic priest and became the head of Charles University in Prague in 1409. A conscientious, dedicated cleric, he was upset by the corruption he saw in the Catholic Church at the time. From the pulpit he challenged the authority and principles of the church and advocated a number of reforms. He spoke up for the right of the people to hear the Mass in their own language rather than in Latin, and to read and interpret the Bible for themselves. He addressed the need to lessen distinctions between the clergy and the laity, including the right of the laity to receive both bread and wine (the body and blood of Christ) in Communion, as opposed to only the bread.

Huss called upon the Church to conduct its affairs in keeping with the teachings of Jesus and to reform itself accordingly. He was censured by the Church and in 1414 was called to a Church council in Constance, Germany, ostensibly to defend his views. Although the council at Constance recognized the need for certain reforms in the Church, they feared that Huss's ideas were too radical. They condemned him as a heretic and offered him two choices: admit his heresy and live out his life in an isolated cell in a Swedish monastery, or die. Huss chose martyrdom, and was burned at the stake in Constance on July 5, 1415. His followers, the Hussites, carried on his ideas in the faith later reborn as the Unitas Fratrum.

John Huss being burned at the stake, from the Jena Codex, produced in Saxony around 1500.

"The first care therefore ought to be of the soul, which is the principal part of man, so that it may become in the highest degree adorned. The next care is for the body that it may be made a habitation fit and worthy of an immortal soul."

John Amos Comenius, The School of Infancy

The History and Faith of the Moravians

View of Herrnhut from the North (detail). Engraving by L. F. Schmutz, Dresden, 1775–1800.

FAITH REBORN AT HERRNHUT

For decades the church survived in small, hidden enclaves in Bohemia, Moravia, and Poland. In 1722 in Dresden, Christian David, a carpenter and a member of the Unity of the Brethren, met Count Nicholas Ludwig von Zinzendorf. During their conversations about religion, David told the count about how the Unity was persecuted and how its members yearned to practice their faith in the light of day. Zinzendorf offered to let a few families settle near his estate at Berthelsdorf, in the German state of Saxony.

Led by Christian David, a small company of Brethren slipped out of Moravia in May 1722. They traveled through Bohemia to Saxony to take sanctuary near Zinzendorf's vast estate. In this refuge, the Moravians gathered strength and built a carefully organized communal town called Herrnhut, a word with two meanings: "under the Lord's watch" and "on watch for the Lord."

A few at a time, other Moravian men, women, and children made their way to Herrnhut, evading their enemies, often crossing unfriendly borders by night. By May 1725 there were ninety Moravians in the Herrnhut community. Other religious refugees also found safety there—Lutherans, Calvinists, Anabaptists, Separatists, and former Catholics. Gradually

Count Zinzendorf assumed the role of minister, counselor, and sometimes mediator to this ecumenical flock.

With the Herrnhutters' varied backgrounds and ideas about how their community should be run, dissension was inevitable. To quell the arguments that were splitting the community, Zinzendorf devised a plan to foster harmony, outlining it in the carefully crafted *Brotherly Agreement of the Brethren from Bohemia and Moravia and Others, Binding Them to Walk According to Apostolic Rule.* This document, which contains many principles of the old Unitas Fratrum, became the foundation for all future Moravian congregation towns, including Salem. It reflected Zinzendorf's long-held belief in being kind to all people, being true to Christ, and carrying the gospel to nonbelievers or the "heathen," as Zinzendorf put it.

ZINZENDORF AND THE MORAVIANS

The goals and practices Zinzendorf laid out fit the traditions the Moravians had brought with them to Herrnhut. He recommended that they live out their faith in every aspect of their daily lives, intermingling the secular and the spiritual. They lived by the teachings and text of the Bible, rather than by the rules handed down by the church hierarchy. They patterned their public worship on the scriptures and the Apostolic Church. They believed in service to the church, to the community, and to the world at large.

In all these beliefs the Moravians were strongly influenced by Pietism, a movement that spread across Europe in the late 1600s and strongly influenced the Lutheran Church. In essence, the Pietists believed in a Christianity of experience and participation, a "heart religion" rather than a rigid doctrine and passive acceptance of a formal creed. Zinzendorf saw the Moravian congregation as a branch of Lutheranism, not as a separate church.

On August 13, 1727, in the beautiful refuge of Herrnhut, the pastor John Andrew Rothe gave an address, after which he, Zinzendorf, and the congregation walked to the Lutheran church in

Berthelsdorf, a mile away. There the congregation took part in a confirmation and communion service led by Pastor John Suss, at which Zinzendorf offered a prayer. The service so inspired the Brethren that Zinzendorf marked it as the spiritual birthday of the Renewed Moravian Church.

A TOWN OF CHOIRS

Herrnhut was located in a German-speaking state, Count Zinzendorf spoke German, and German quickly became the common language of the Herrnhut Moravian community. At its height, Herrnhut was a good-sized, beautifully ordered town of two hundred houses. Its communal society was governed by a council of twelve elders that administered every detail of the town, from education to health care to municipal services to the personal lives of the residents. The elders oversaw a man or woman's choice of trade or occupation and the choice of a spouse, as well. They also oversaw each congregation member's spiritual growth.

The congregation was divided into small *Bunden*, or bands of members. This system was later supplanted by an organized system of *choirs*. Most people think of a choir as a group of people who sing or play musical instruments. The Moravians loved music and used the word *choir* in this way, but they also used it in another sense. For them a choir was also a particular group within the church congregation that was bonded by age, gender, or marital status. Its members came together for spiritual growth as well as for sharing certain responsibilities of life within the church and the community.

In Herrnhut there was a choir of Married Brothers and a choir of Married Sisters. In addition, there were choirs composed of Single Brothers, Single Sisters, Widowers, Widows, Older Boys, Older Girls, Little Boys and Little Girls, and Infants. The choirs met almost daily, and choir leaders watched over the spiritual growth of each member.

All Moravian towns in the eighteenth and early nineteenth centuries followed the choir system, with variations. In Salem there were choirs of Married People, Single Sisters, Single Brothers, Widows, Widowers, Older Girls, Older Boys, and Little Girls and Little Boys. In Bethabara and Bethania, perhaps because of smaller numbers, little boys and little girls were combined into one Children's Choir.

The History and Faith of the Moravians

The choirs were modified to fit the needs of the congregation towns at different times. Herrnhut and Bethlehem, Pennsylvania, were the only towns to have an Infants' Choir. This was a nursery established to care for babies whose parents had been dispatched to serve the Moravian Church in other cities, even other countries. When Brother and Sister Johann Michael Graff were called to North America in 1762, they left their infant daughter Justine in the nursery in Herrnhut. The Graffs lived in Salem, where they died without ever seeing their daughter again.

Unmarried men and older boys lived together in the Single Brothers' House, while unmarried women and older girls shared the Single Sisters' House. Each group had its own leaders who played an important role in the congregation. Education was a primary concern for the community. Girls as well as boys were educated, which was an uncommon practice for the time. Elsewhere, only girls from upper-class families had the privilege of formal schooling. Older boys and girls learned useful work, from spinning, weaving, carpentry, and joining, to farming and cooking.

There were daily church services in Herrnhut, and Moravians often attended more than one service a day. Music and

Count Nicholas von Zinzendorf

Count Nicholas Ludwig von Zinzendorf was born on May 26, 1700, into one of the twelve noble houses that constituted the Austrian dynasty. Raised in a pious Lutheran household and rigorously educated, he wanted to devote his life to God from an early age. This shocked his family, who did not see the ministry as an appropriate career for a nobleman.

In 1722 he married Dorothea von Reuss and on their estate at Berthelsdorf, they formed a religious community where they could practice their beliefs. This became the town of Herrnhut, where the Moravians revived their church under Zinzendorf's leadership.

Zinzendorf was a gifted speaker, and his discussions of faith and redemption inspired many to join the community at Herrnhut. In 1734, Zinzendorf was ordained a minister in the Lutheran Church; he became a Moravian bishop in 1737.

After years of criticism by the Saxon government and nobility, Zinzendorf was exiled from Saxony in 1736. He founded a new settlement near Frankfurt, called Herrnhaag. From there he traveled widely. In 1747 he was allowed to return to Herrnhut. He continued to travel, however, using London as his base of operations from 1749 to 1755. During the years of travel and exile, his wife Dorothea kept his affairs in order, sometimes traveling with him but usually staying in Herrnhut or Herrnhaag. She died in Herrnhut in 1756. In 1757, Zinzendorf married Sister Anna Nitschmann, who had assisted him in church matters for years. He died at Herrnhut on May 9, 1760.

Sister Anna Nitschmann

Anna Nitschmann's service to Moravian Church congregations in Europe and abroad demonstrates the weight women carried in Moravian society. Sister Nitschmann was a talented leader who, when only fourteen, had been elected by Lot as the chief eldress at Herrnhut. For a short time when she was eighteen, she served as head of the church there.

Sister Nitschmann organized the very first choir of Single Sisters when she was fourteen, and she played a vital role in the Pilgrim Congregation working in North America. During her short tenure as chief eldress of the church, she presided over meetings, cast the deciding vote on issues before the church council, and administered the parting blessing to the dying. During the time of Zinzendorf's exile from Herrnhut, Sister Anna accompanied him on his travels from one outpost of the church to another.

In 1741 Bishop Spangenberg observed the various factions that threatened the solid foundation of the Pennsylvania settlement and decided that only a woman could win the trust and cooperation of the people. He believed that with her sweet, friendly nature and her gentle diplomacy, Sister Anna Nitschmann would work wonders. She served for two years in Pennsylvania, greatly facilitating the effective organization of the congregations.

A year after Countess Erdmuth Dorothea died in 1756, Zinzendorf married Anna. After three years of marriage, the count and his new wife died within two weeks of each other in 1760. He was sixty and she was forty-five.

prayers punctuated the daily routine. Count Zinzendorf not only composed hymns, but he started the ritual of choosing a verse of scripture as the daily text or watchword for the community, a practice that continues today.

A distinctive aspect of Moravian worship is the lovefeast, a service based on the early Christian agape meal. It combines singing and scripture with a simple meal of coffee or tea and special rolls, which were shared in a spirit of joy and thanksgiving. Among the early Moravians, lovefeasts were held to give thanks and to celebrate important occasions such as a religious holiday, the completion of a new building, the arrival of an important visitor, or a choir's festival day. Today the Christmas lovefeast is an important Moravian tradition.

In the structure of their town and their religious beliefs, the Moravians were challenging the status quo. When Count Zinzendorf was exiled by the government of Saxony in 1736 for his religious beliefs, he took this as an opportunity to spread the Moravian faith. He and a group of trusted church members established Moravian settlements in England, Ireland, Holland, Berlin, Russia, and Switzerland, as well as in the New World.

Zinzendorf himself traveled widely to oversee and inspire his flock. While living in London, he and his followers established several Moravian communities in England. In 1738, he traveled to the mission fields in the West Indies, where he was impressed by what the missionaries had accomplished.

In December 1741, accompanied by his eldest daughter Anna Benigna and others, he came by ship to Pennsylvania. On that Christmas Eve, he gave the Moravian congregation at Bethlehem its name. On the same trip, he set guidelines for the government of the Moravian Church in America and ventured into Indian territory to plan missionary endeavors among the Native Americans.

Even after Zinzendorf's death in 1760, the Moravian Church continued to grow and flourish around the world. It would be guided by a basic precept that reflected the count's ideals: "In essentials, Unity; in nonessentials, Liberty; in all things, Love."

Portrait of Anna Nitschmann, attributed to Johann Valentin Haidt, c.1750

"Did you suppose, in the beginning, that the Savior would do as much as we now really see, in the various Moravian settlements, amongst the children of God of other denominations, and amongst the heathen? I only entreated of him a few of the firstfruits [sic] of the latter, but there are now thousands of them. Nitschmann, what a formidable caravan from our church already stands around the Lamb!"

Count Zinzendorf to his brother-in-law, Brother David Nitschmann, on the day before the count died.

This 1775 Fraktur, or illuminated document, shows the various Moravian settlements, missions, and societies from around the world as the fruits on a healthy, spreading grape vine. It was painted by P. J. Ferber in Herrnhut for Frederic William Marshall.

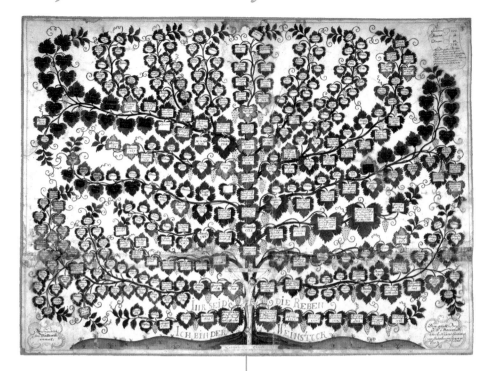

MORAVIAN MISSIONARIES PLANT THE SEED OF FAITH

"I leave it to the good judgment of the congregation and have no other ground than this thought: that on the island there are souls who cannot believe because they have not heard." With these words, Brother Leonard Dober set sail in 1732 for St. Thomas in the Danish West Indies as one of the first two Moravian missionaries. The other was David Nitschmann.

Since 1708 or 1709, Count Zinzendorf had felt what he called a "missionary impulse." As a result, spreading the word of God became a cornerstone of the Moravian Church. The Moravians did not strive to convert others to their religion, but to deepen the faith of believers and to introduce nonbelievers to God.

In Denmark in 1731, Zinzendorf met Anthony Ulrich, an enslaved African from St. Thomas who had become a convert to Christianity. Ulrich spoke to the count of the need for spiritual guidance among the enslaved people on his island, and urged him to send a preacher there. Dober and Nitschmann volunteered to go to St. Thomas in 1732. It was to be the Moravian's first encounter with a society and an economy dependent on the labor of enslaved Africans.

Over time the Moravians converted thirteen thousand enslaved Africans in the West Indies. Their work was to love and serve the people who, despite the secular repression of their freedom and dignity, were their spiritual brothers and sisters. Through these missionary efforts, many of the Moravians who came to North Carolina understood the workings of a slave-based economy. Like other church groups, they bent religious dogma to economic purpose to rationalize the moral and spiritual ramifications of slavery.

The Moravians sent missionaries to Greenland in 1733; to Lapland in 1734; to Surinam and to the colony of Georgia in 1735; to the Guinea Coast of Africa in 1736; to South Africa in 1737; to the Jewish quarter of Amsterdam in 1738; to Algeria in 1739; and, in 1740, to the North American Indians, to Constantinople and Ceylon, and to Romania.

Other eighteenth-century mission settlements were located in Baghdad, Cairo, and Jerusalem, and at various sites in South America, South Africa, the West Indies, and North America. By 1742, more than 70 of the 600 Moravians from Herrnhut had braved the dangers of travel and the hazards of the unknown to work as missionaries around the globe. By 1832, a century after Brothers Dober and Nitschmann traveled to St. Thomas, there were forty-two Moravian mission sites around the world.

The Moravians Come to North America

Early in the 1730s, the Moravians resolved to spread the Gospel to the native peoples of North America. They founded a settlement in Georgia in 1733, but abandoned it in 1740 rather than bear arms in the ongoing border disputes between the English and the Spanish. Besides, these sturdy, determined Brethren were worn down by tropical disease and weather and by the animosity of other settlers in the Georgia colony.

In 1740–41 the Moravians established the town of Bethlehem, Pennsylvania, which was to be the administrative center of church operations in North America. In the early years in Bethlehem, Moravians were trained to be teachers and missionaries. Many of them established missions among Native Americans, first in New York and Pennsylvania, and then farther west. Other Moravian towns in Pennsylvania were established in the eighteenth century, including Nazareth and Lititz.

As their reputation as conscientious, industrious, peaceable colonists spread, John Carteret, the Earl of Granville, a Proprietor of the Royal Province of North Carolina, offered to sell the Moravians one hundred thousand acres of his Caro-

lina land. In 1752, they decided to do so. Their intentions were no doubt secular as well as spiritual: it not only expanded their opportunities to work with Native Americans, but the geographical expansion of the church also opened the way for a stronger economic foundation. When Bishop August Spangenberg and a small band of Moravian men set out in August to choose land in the Carolina wilderness, they traveled by horseback and boat from

(Above)
Careful attention to the town plan and sturdy construction methods were already in evidence in Bethlehem, the first Moravian congregation town in North America.

Nicholas Garrison, View of Bethlehem, Pennsylvania, 1750–1760

(Left)
Moravians established six missions in Greenland; New Herrnhut, settled in 1738 was the first.

Christian Gottlieb Reuter, New Herrnhut in Greenland, 1761.

15

Exploring North Carolina

The Wachovia Tract in North Carolina, as drawn by surveyor Christian Gottlieb Reuter in 1766.

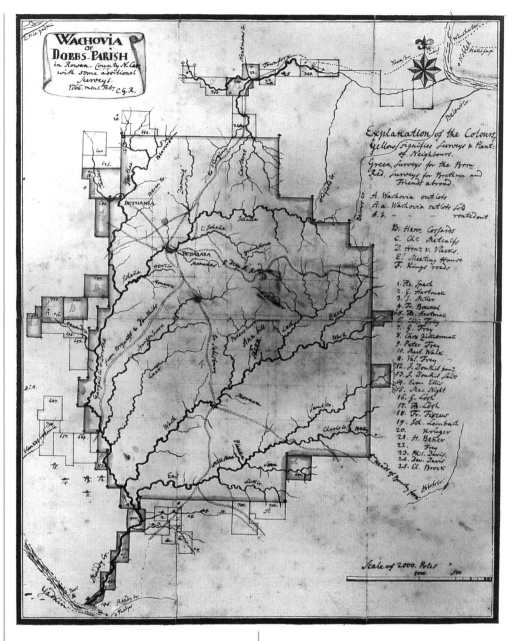

"On the 27th [of August, 1752], we called on Mr. Daniel Benezet's brother-in-law in Philadelphia to inquire about conditions in Carolina, and the best way to reach there, since he had stayed for a time in Edenton. His information was not encouraging."

Bishop Spangenberg Diary

from Bethlehem to Edenton, North Carolina, a journey that lasted until September 10, 1752. They spent the next four and a half months exploring the rugged backcountry Carolina wilderness, with Spangenberg tracking their progress and their adventures in careful entries in his diary.

In December, after a hunter serving as their guide missed a mountain trail, the party struggled over rugged cliffs and mountains, sometimes on their hands and knees. Their horses, Spangenberg wrote, "were trembling like a leaf." At the top of the Blue Ridge Mountains, near the modern towns of Blowing Rock and Boone, North Carolina, the weary broth-

ers "saw mountains to right and to left, before and behind us, many hundreds of mountains, rising like great waves in a storm."

Ever philosophical, however, the brothers rejoiced a few weeks later when they reached a tract of land in the Piedmont at the three forks of Muddy Creek, also called Carguel's Creek. Spangenberg described the land they discovered there as probably the best unsettled tract left in North Carolina.

The Moravian explorers were certain that this newly discovered land had been "reserved by the Lord for the Brethren." Bishop Spangenberg and his companions all rejoiced in the "countless springs, and

Bishop August G. Spangenberg

One of the most beloved figures in Moravian history, Bishop Spangenberg was also known as Brother Joseph for his role in protecting his people in strange lands.

The youngest of four brothers, August Gottlieb Spangenberg was only a year old when his mother died. His father, a Lutheran minister, died before August Gottlieb was ten. An intensely spiritual child, he was educated in an orphan school. He went on to secure a university education and a post as a university teacher. During this time he met Count Zinzendorf and several Herrnhuters and first learned about the Unity of the Brethren.

Spangenberg joined the church in 1733 and quickly became one of Zinzendorf's most trusted advisers and administrators. He was a practical, fair-minded man who won the enduring respect and affection of his colleagues. The count chose Spangenberg to lead the Moravian expedition to Georgia and to participate in the evangelical work of the Pennsylvania settlement. In later years, he wrote a biography of Zinzendorf, as well as a theological guide to the Moravian Church and several books for children.

Spangenberg was married twice, the second time to the mother of Matthew Miksch. In 1744 he became a bishop in charge of the Moravian Church in North America. After Count Zinzendorf's death in 1760, he assumed a leading role in the Unitas Fratrum. In 1792 Brother Spangenberg died at the age of eighty-eight and was laid to rest at Herrnhut.

numerous fine creeks," where "as many mills as may be desired can be built." Spangenberg wrote in his diary of abundant "beautiful meadow land" and "good pasturage for cattle," as well as promising farmland. The hills were gentle, the air "fresh and healthful," and the springs and streams plentiful and good. The forest seemed ripe with game to "help supply the table of the first settlers," but the services of a "good, true, untiring, trustworthy forester and hunter" would certainly be required because "the wolves and bears must be exterminated if cattle raising is to succeed."

The Moravians purchased fourteen adjoining pieces of land in this tract, and Spangenberg named it *Wachau* after the Zinzendorf family estate in Austria. "Why should we not call it Wachau," he wrote, "and so renew that name." The word means "meadow along the Wach," a stream flowing through the Wachau valley in Austria. Later, the name was changed to the Latinized *Wachovia*.

By the time all negotiations had been completed, Wachovia comprised 98,985 acres of land, at the center of which Salem would eventually be built. In the twentieth century, Wachovia would be the site of modern-day Winston-Salem and the core of Forsyth County, North Carolina.

But first came Bethabara.

(Above) Spangenberg's field notes for December 6, 1752, in which he describes coming upon the tract of land the Moravians would buy from Lord Granville.

(Left) Portrait of August Gottlieb Spangenberg, attributed to Johann Georg Ziesensis, c.1770.

Bethabara

Christian Gottlieb Reuter, Map of Bethabara in 1766.

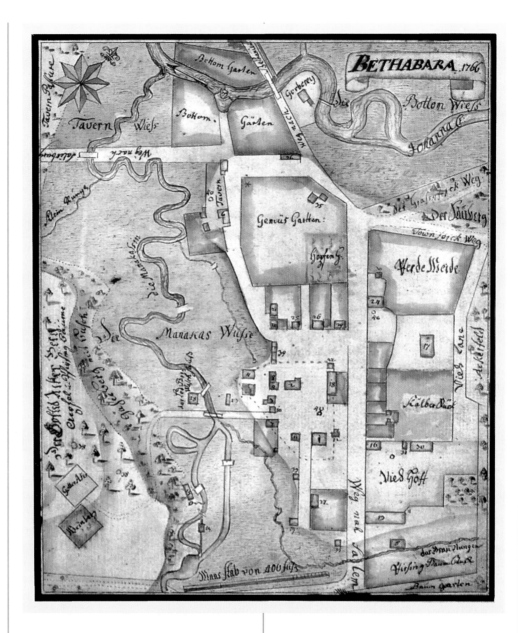

"While we held our Lovefeast the wolves howled loudly, but all was well with us, and our hearts were full of thanksgiving to the Savior Who had so graciously guided and led us. Then we laid ourselves down to rest, and Br. Gottlob Konigsdorfer hung his hammock above our heads."

Bethabara Diary, November 17, 1753

"In the evening there was a Lovefeast in which we reviewed the difficult beginnings, and the successful progress in the Wachau, thanking the Father and Lord Whom we serve. Br. Marshall took this occasion to announce that the founding of a new town in Wachovia was the chief object of his visit."

Bethabara Diary November 17, 1764

Early in October 1753, fifteen unmarried Moravian men were chosen to travel from Pennsylvania to the new land in Carolina. Each brought essential skills to the challenge of carving a settlement out of the wilderness. There was a minister who could cook and garden; a business manager; a surgeon; a shoemaker who was a sick-nurse; and one brother who was not only a farmer, but also a shoemaker, carpenter, mill-wright, cooper, sievemaker, and turner!

This "little Pilgrim Band," as one brother described them, reached the Wachovia tract in North Carolina soon after noon on November 17, 1753. According to the Wachovia Diary for that year, they "cut a road for two and a half miles" to an abandoned cabin two of the Brethren had discovered the preceding day. They celebrated their safe arrival with a lovefeast and named their settlement Bethabara, meaning "house of passage." From the first, this site was meant to be the way station to the permanent congregation town that would be called Salem.

The Bethabara pilgrims set to work immediately. They cleared land, planted crops, built a bake-oven and furniture, bought livestock from farmers in nearby settlements, and established a mill site. In the diary they kept, they celebrated their good fortune in owning "unusually good land" with "especially fine meadows."

Their numbers gradually grew as more men and, from November 1755, married couples, came from Pennsylvania. Bethabara was to be run as an *Oeconomie,* a communal system of common housekeeping and labor. Under the Oeconomie, Single Sisters lived together in one house, and Single Brothers in another. Several married couples shared a household as well. The community was carefully structured so that all things operated for the common good. This efficient community organization provided everything the settlers needed: food, lodging, simple but beautifully crafted furniture, ceramic wares and tile stoves, and woven goods. By 1759 the Bethabara settlement had grown to be the home of seventy-three people.

The peace-loving Moravians were determined to expand their settlement, build a central town, and minister to the Cherokee Indians, but their religious mission was forcibly disrupted by the French and Indian War from 1754 to 1760. During the war, Bethabara provided a safe haven for other settlers. A palisade was erected at Bethabara in 1755, and ten houses were built nearby to shelter refugees. Even after the official end of the French and Indian War, reports reached Wachovia of skirmishes along the Catawba River between the settlers and "Northern Indians."

Unfortunately, the war years had interrupted the hoped-for growth in population in Wachovia. There was simply more work to be done in Wachovia than there were workers to do it. Beginning in 1755, the Moravians hired outsiders to help them with their work in Bethabara. By fall 1762, fifteen people were working for hire in Bethabara, and in 1763 thirty-six hired laborers helped gather the fall harvest. It was expensive to pay these workers, however, and the frugal, practical Moravians realized that it would be cheaper to rent slave labor than to engage the services of free men and women.

The Moravians in eighteenth-century North America, whether in Bethlehem or in Wachovia, did not object to slavery in principle. They did not yet perceive a conflict between professing Christian beliefs and owning or renting slaves. In August 1763, as the labor shortage worsened, the Moravians decided to lease enslaved workers from some of their neighbors who were not members of the Moravian Church. Franke, an African American

woman, was hired for a three-year term to work as a maid in the Bethabara Tavern. By 1767, Franke's rheumatism kept her from working effectively, and the Moravians rented the labor of Cate, a young African-American woman.

A second community, Bethania, was established in 1759 for those Moravians impatient to have their own households and their own farmland. It was located three miles north of Bethabara. Despite their close proximity, the two towns were quite different. In Bethania, families owned their own homes and ran their households, businesses, and farms independently, rather than as part of the Oeconomie.

Relying on accounts from travelers and from letters, the Moravians in Wachovia anxiously followed the progress of the Seven Years' War in Europe. At last, on February 10, 1763, England and Portugal signed a peace treaty with France and Spain; in the same month Austria and Prussia made peace, ending a worldwide conflict that touched even remote wilderness settlements such as Wachovia. In their church records for the year, leaders of the Moravians in Wachovia wrote, "The struggle has lasted nearly seven years, has spread into all parts of the world, has cost the lives of a million men, and many cities and towns are ruined."

In November 1764, Frederic Marshall arrived in Bethabara. The Moravians celebrated the eleventh anniversary of the first settlers' arrival in Wachovia. Brother Marshall brought good news: planning the new town of Salem was finally to begin.

The 1787 Gemeinhaus at Bethabara is an outstanding example of eighteenth-century Moravian architecture in North America. Today Bethabara is an archaeological park that displays several features from the early settlement.

"Bethania now has ten houses. Half belong to the Brethren the others to neighbors who have placed themselves under the care of the Brethren and have been formed into a Society."

Letter from Bishop Spangenberg to Count Zinzendorf, written from Bethlehem, Pennsylvania, June 11, 1760.

2. Planning and Building Salem

"Br. Frederic Marshall was put in charge of affairs in Wachovia by the Herrnhut Board, with Br. Ettwein as his local representative. The Board also instructed Br. Marshall to select a suitable site for a central town, and to decide whether work on it should be begun at once."

Wachovia Church Book, 1763

The Moravians who cut the timbers and laid the foundation stones for the first houses in Salem were building far more than the eye could see. With the guidance of the church council in Herrnhut, Germany, they hoped to build an idealistic community where people lived together in harmony, serving God and each other. Their careful design for Salem grew out of the broad vision of the church in Europe and North America and was tailored by Brother Frederic William Marshall to surmount the challenges of the Carolina wilderness.

According to the Moravians in Herrnhut, the plans for the new town in Wachovia were ordained by God. Salem would be an ideal community founded on religious principles, and inhabited by men and women who lived out those principles in every part of their daily lives. It would be a congregation town whose citizens would live and work together as a family. The church would oversee the spiritual and secular life of each man, woman, and child. On a practical level, Salem would be the center for Wachovia's commerce, trades, and professions. These were the dreams undergirding the first sturdy houses and buildings that the Moravians erected in Salem beginning in 1766.

During the 1750s, as Count Zinzendorf envisioned a central town for Wachovia, he first called it Unitas, but by 1756 he had chosen the biblical name Salem, which means "peace." The new town of Salem would serve several functions. It would be the seat of governance for the Wachovia settlement and a center for trade and industry in North Carolina and the Southeast. It would also be a vital link in the hierarchy of the international Unity of Brethren, connecting the Moravians in the South, those inhabiting the Pennsylvania settlement, and those dwelling in Herrnhut. It would expand the worldwide outreach of the church. It would also be a utopian community in which each member should feel called by God to live in this special place.

BROTHER MARSHALL AND HIS PLAN FOR SALEM

In 1763 the church appointed an *oeconomus*, or chief officer for financial and other business affairs, for Wachovia. The person they chose was Frederic William Marshall. Minister, administrator, city planner, diplomat, orator, Frederic Marshall is a pivotal figure in Moravian history. He was born on February 5, 1721, near Dresden and died in Salem on February 11, 1802. He came to North America in 1761

Portrait of Frederic William Marshall, late eighteenth century, artist unknown. Pencil drawing on paper.

Sister Elisabeth Marshall

Hedwig Elizabeth von Schweinitz Marshall was a Moravian personage in her own right, as well as a full partner in her husband's achievements. Her remarkable life of leadership and service was foreshadowed in earliest childhood. She was born into an aristocratic family in Leube, Germany, in 1724. When Count Zinzendorf came to Leube in 1729, little Elizabeth attended his children's class; she was enchanted by his words and the faith he described. She met other Moravians in her father's home, and by the time she was twelve, she wanted to join the Unity of Brethren. She and her sister persuaded their father to move the family to Herrnhut in 1737.

After her father's death in 1740, Elizabeth began working energetically for the congregation in Herrnhut, where she grew close to the Zinzendorf family. She lived with them in Herrnhaag, where Count Zinzendorf adopted her. She served in the Pilgrim Congregation in London, was ordained as a deaconess, and was later appointed leader of the Single Sisters at Herrnhut.

Frederic William Marshall was also part of the Zinzendorf household. When Elizabeth was in her mid-twenties, Count Zinzendorf decided that Frederic Marshall would be a worthy match for her. The two were married June 30, 1750. They had two daughters, born in 1752 and 1754, and a son who died in 1764 at the age of two.

Elizabeth was a resilient woman of robust energy, passionate devotion to church and family, and a lively temper. She possessed another trait that served her well—she never got seasick. She and her husband would, all told, spend more than a year of their lives at sea in their travels and pilgrimages on behalf of the church. They sailed for North America in 1761.

Elizabeth Marshall spent the final twenty-seven years of her life in the Wachovia settlement. As the revered leader of the women of Salem and all of Wachovia, she dispensed advice, sympathy, and practical assistance. Mama Marshall, as she came to be called, was much admired for her compassion for the needy. Her memoir states, "She had put aside the prerogatives of her rank & rather familiarized herself with the poor."

Sadly, Sister Elizabeth did not live to see her husband's last great project—the design and construction of Home Moravian Church in 1800. She was "called home," as the Moravians described death, on March 22, 1795.

to oversee the financial and business affairs of Moravian congregations in the New World, and from 1763, the planning, financing, and building of Salem.

As a bright, ambitious young university student in Leipzig, Marshall heard Count Zinzendorf speak. Marshall was so impressed that he abandoned his goal of a military career to follow, as he later wrote, "a clear call to the service of the Savior." In 1740 Marshall joined the Unity of the Brethren, and in 1741 went to London to help Zinzendorf found the first settlement in England. In 1742, he witnessed the sailing of the Sea Congregation, the band of Moravians who set out to build the Pennsylvania settlement.

Count Zinzendorf was greatly impressed with Marshall's talents and character, and Marshall became a member of Zinzendorf's household. He advised the count on business matters, helped oversee building projects, and traveled widely among the Moravian congregations in England. In 1750, he married Zinzendorf's adopted daughter, Hedwig Elizabeth von Scheweinitz, who became an active partner in his responsibilities and his travels.

In Wachovia, true to Count Zinzendorf's vision, the church oversaw both spiritual and secular matters. By the time Brother Marshall came to Wachovia, there were four boards in place that managed the affairs of the Moravians. The Elders' Conference, or *Aeltesten Conferenz*, was composed of ministers, their wives, and

This row of half-timbered houses, built between 1766 and 1768, gives us a glimpse of one of the first streetscapes in Salem.

Privately occupied.

"In every duty to which I was called my dear wife was a faithful and diligent helpmeet, with counsel, assistance and comfort for spiritual and material needs, and in the almost 45 years of our marriage . . . I knew no other attendant or nurse, for she did all for me herself."

Frederic Marshall

21

Planning and Building Salem

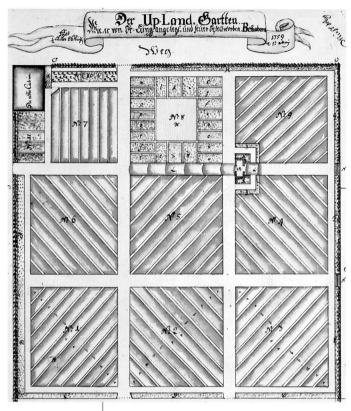

Plan of the Upland Garden at Bethabara, by Christian Gottlieb Reuter, 1759

"As I stepped on Wachovia ground, I felt very good and thought:

This is the Savior's land, now I am going to be His Surveyor."

Christian Gottlieb Reuter, Memoir

other church officials. They supervised and mediated all moral and religious matters. The Board of Supervisors, or *Aufseher Collegium*, oversaw the finances and other material business of the congregation, and regulated the trades and professions. Because the Moravians believed this to be men's work, no women served on this board, although the choir of Single Sisters was represented by a man, called a *Curator*. The Congregation Council, or *Gemein Rath*, governed such community business as church fees, major building projects, and new roads. It was made up of the Elders Conference and the Board of Supervisors, as well as elected representatives of all the adult choirs in the Congregation. The Helpers' Conference, or *Helfer Conferenz*, was an advisory board that kept watch over all Unity affairs and all matters involving the Salem, Bethabara, and Bethania congregations. Its mission was later expanded to embrace all of Wachovia.

By the time that the church council in Herrnhut and the leaders of Wachovia began to plan Salem, they could draw on lessons learned at Herrnhut and other congregation towns. The planners of Salem benefitted greatly from the knowledge of what had succeeded and what had

Christian Gottlieb Reuter

For all of its emphasis on communal living and conformity, Salem was a town full of unique individuals. One of the most memorable is Christian Gottlieb Reuter, who was not only a skilled and trusted surveyor and forester, but a talented mapmaker, botanist, naturalist, and poet. His maps and plans are the best sources of information we have about the early years in Wachovia.

Brother Reuter was born in Prussia on September 5, 1717. Raised a Lutheran, he converted to the Moravian faith in 1744. In 1756, after having worked as a surveyor in Herrnhut, Brother Reuter was called by the church to go to North America. For the first year and a half he worked in Moravian towns in Pennsylvania. In June 1758, Reuter moved to Bethabara and began to map the 154 square miles of wilderness that made up the Wachovia tract. He spent four years compiling meticulous records of the land, its streams and waterways, and the flora and fauna that flourished there. At the end of that time, in addition to numerous other maps and plans, he produced the richly detailed Wachovia Great Map, seven by nine feet in size.

In 1772, Reuter moved to Salem with his wife Anna Catherina Antes Kalberlahn, whom he had married in 1762. The couple was active in Salem life. Brother Reuter was appointed to the Committee of Arbitrators, or community court, and was made road-master and chief forester, a critical job as building in Salem increased. He and Sister Reuter both served as *Saal Diener,* or sextons. Sister Reuter was a member of the Helpers' Conference and performed other functions for the church as well.

The congregation relied heavily on Brother Reuter's expertise as a surveyor, his remarkably accurate maps, and his commitment to the church. For Reuter, each lonely, methodical trek through the wilderness, each plant or tree cited, each ridge and stream recorded meant more than geography, cartography, and botany. He was doing the Lord's work in Wachovia, exploring and helping to open consecrated land.

When illness made it impossible for Brother Reuter to walk the land he loved and knew so well, he began to teach Ludwig Meinung the art of surveying. Reuter died in December 1777 at the age of sixty.

failed to work in those settlements.

As was the case in Herrnhut, Bethabara, and other Moravian towns, the residents of Salem would be organized into choirs. The Single Sisters' and the Single Brothers' choirs would eventually own the buildings that were especially designed and built for their residences and their workshops. The congregation would own and operate most of Salem's major businesses and industries—the town store, the pottery, the tannery, the tavern, and the mill. The congregation also set all wages, regulated all trades and industries, and owned all land. Town lots were leased to congregation members who could, with council approval, build houses or business structures on the land. The individual leaseholder owned the buildings on the land he leased, while the church continued to own the land itself. In this way, the church maintained control over town life.

CHOOSING A SITE

Finding the right location for Salem was not an easy task. It needed good farmland, access to water for drinking and for powering mills, and abundant forests to provide building materials. In addition, the site needed to be approved by the Lot (see right) to be sure that it was chosen according to God's plan. Although Christian Gottlieb Reuter, a trained and highly skilled surveyor, had earlier surveyed the Wachovia tract and helped to choose the general site for a central town, Brother Marshall and other brethren spent three months searching for just the right location within that site.

At last, in February 1765, helped by two weeks of unusually mild weather, Marshall and the brothers settled on two suitable locations for Salem. On February 14 they submitted the question to the Lot for the final decision. By this time Marshall and the elders had already consulted the Lot five times, only to receive a negative answer to all other possible sites for the new town.

On the night of the decisive Lot, the elders wrote out three slips of paper, one with "Site no. 1," another with "Site no. 2," and a third left blank. The Lot for Site no. 2 was drawn. It was the ridge of land

A Lot bowl used in early Salem, with the tubes used to hold the slips of paper that were drawn from the bowl.

between the Petersbach (now Peter's Creek) and the Wach, which Brothers Marshall and Ettwein had visited several times. The Moravians were happy with the site and glad to have the matter settled. The next day, three brothers visited the newly chosen ground for Salem and began to blaze the first pathway to it.

THE LOT

The Moravians used the Lot to determine God's will in spiritual and secular matters. This practice was based on biblical references contained in Numbers 33:54 and Acts 1:26. Neither a lottery nor a random act of drawing straws, the Lot was a ritual of serious, sacred significance. Only the church board of elders was authorized to use it.

After the elders had done everything possible to reach a sound conclusion about what should be done in a matter—in this case, which site should be chosen for the new town—two or three outcomes, or Lots, were written on slips of paper, encased in slender tubes cut from reeds, and placed in the Lot bowl. Often, one slip bore the word *ja*, or "yes," and another *nein*, or "no." A third slip was left blank, meaning that more prayer and deliberation were needed. One Lot was then solemnly drawn from the bowl, and the answer it gave was heeded. Sometimes scripture verses would be inscribed on

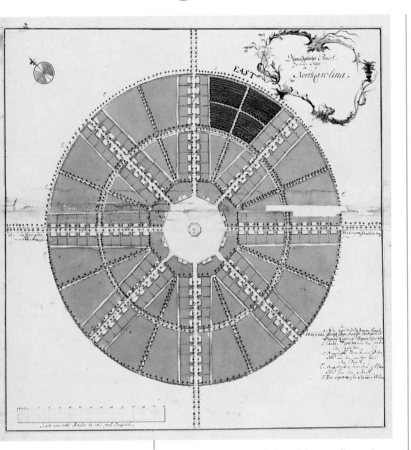

and curving streams of North Carolina.

After the site for Salem was selected, Brother Marshall and Wachovia's surveyor, Christian Gottlieb Reuter, began a more practical design for Salem that would fit the ridges and hollows of the chosen land. The layout was similar to that of congregation towns in Lititz, Pennsylvania, and Niesky and Gnadenberg in Germany. It was a symmetrical plan with a town square at the center, streets laid out on a grid, and one main street running the length of the ridge. Marshall drew in cross streets and sited certain key buildings—the *Gemein Haus*, or congregational meeting house; the *Saal*, or hall for religious services; the Boys' School; the Girls' School; the town store; and the houses for Single Sisters and Single Brothers.

Meticulously, Marshall considered every detail of daily life in drawing up this plan, from the size of the lots and the width of the streets to the distances each resident would have to walk to church. He wanted families to live in separate houses when at all possible, with lots deep enough for family gardens. He wanted children to have room for "their recreations under oversight." While Marshall made it clear that the new town was "not designed for farmers, but for those with trades," at the beginning he wanted families to be able to grow some of their own food, both in gardens and in outlots, or small plantations, outside the town.

WORK BEGINS ON THE NEW TOWN

The Moravians set out to build Salem in their typical orderly, faithful way. They recorded each setback or step forward in the Bethabara Diary for 1766. On February 19, after their planned departure for Salem had been delayed for nine days because of a fierce snowstorm, eight Single Brothers struck out from Bethabara to "begin active work in Salem." The company included four Brethren who had just arrived from Europe: Nils Petersen, a brewer, and Jens Schmidt, an anchorsmith, both from Denmark; Gottfried Praetzel, a weaver from Germany; and John Birkhead, from England, who had worked in a cloth factory. With them were Jacob Steiner, a miller; George Holder, a

Zinzendorf's plan for the town of Salem, by an unknown artist, 1755 or 1756. This idealized plan, in which all roads lead to the church at the center of the town, had administrative buildings, house lots, pastures and fields, and a graveyard (in green). Unfortunately, the plan was not suited to the rugged terrain of the North Carolina piedmont.

slips of paper, and the elders reflected on how the verse chosen could illuminate their decision.

The Lot was also used to make decisions about choosing a pastor, electing elders, accepting individuals into the congregation, choosing partners in marriage, and selecting a person's trade or profession. In 1818, the church stopped using the Lot to determine marriage partners for congregation members who were not ministers. From that time until 1889, the use of the Lot was systematically eliminated as a way of making decisions about church matters.

THE TOWN PLAN

Back in 1755, Count Zinzendorf had conceived a plan for the new central town. The count, who never traveled to Wachovia, envisioned a spacious town laid out in a circular design over 380 acres of land, with the congregation church standing in the center of eight wide boulevards. While Zinzendorf's communal vision could be applied to Salem's social structure, his physical plan for the town could not have been imposed on the dense forests, sloping hills, farmer; master mason Melchior Rasp, who was born in Germany; and Michael Ziegler, who eventually drifted away from the Moravian Church.

For the trip to Salem, the Brothers packed two wagons with bedding and cooking equipment, along with roofing tiles and bricks for building a chimney, all made in Bethabara. On the way they shot two deer to provision their new kitchen. Surveyor Reuter went along to establish the sites for the square and the streets, "running the lines for two main streets along the ridge," and laying off "several squares 400 by 300 feet, one of which was to be selected for the Square."

During March, fields were cleared and plowed, peach and apple trees were planted, and trees were cut and hewn into logs to build a cabin for "stranger workmen," non-Moravians who would be hired to help with the construction. On April 12, 1766, the town square was measured off at 380 feet long and 300 feet wide; building lots were laid out for the next houses to be constructed; and the site for the graveyard, to be called God's Acre, was chosen.

With these plans laid, the Moravians embarked on a formidable building campaign that lasted until 1772, constructing the main administrative buildings and a number of houses that would serve as private family dwellings and workshops. Once building began in earnest, there was a steady flow of wagons and horses between Bethabara and Salem. With obligations in Bethabara and Bethania as well as Salem, the Moravians were more short-handed than ever. They could not work as fast as they had hoped that first year, despite the hired help of outsiders. They brought in construction workers, including brickmasons and stonemasons.

Even in these early days, the growth of Salem and the other towns in the settlement depended on the contributions of African Americans, whether free or enslaved. As work in Salem progressed, the Moravians rented enslaved Africans to work as teamsters and to help with building. The church elders also began to buy slaves on behalf of the congregation—Frank, a mason's assistant in 1771, for instance, and Sambo, a tanner's assistant, as well as a procession of other men, wom-

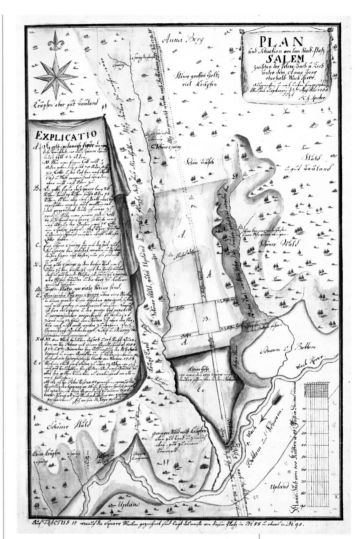

en, and children. By the early 1770s, according to some estimates, there were about twenty-five Africans and African Americans in Wachovia, compared to the white population of about two hundred.

MOVING TO SALEM

In the lush Carolina spring of 1772, when most of the primary buildings of the town were ready for occupancy, 120 people moved from Bethabara to Salem. They included nineteen married couples, two widows, forty-three Single Brothers and older boys, twenty-two Single Sisters and older girls, and fifteen children. They busily settled into life in their private houses, the Single Brothers' House, and the Gemeinhaus. Once the trades and professions, along with the church offices, were moved to the town, Salem officially became the center of the Moravian settlement of Wachovia.

The plan of Salem drawn by Christian Gottlieb Reuter in 1765 according to Frederic Marshall's ideas. This plan reflects the reality of the site the Moravians chose—the high ridge along which the main road runs, the streams, and the abundant forests that would provide a source of timber for building. The square, shown here straddling the road, was actually placed on the east side of Main Street.

25

Salem Square

View of Salem Square, watercolor by Elias Vogler c.1837–1847

The reconstructed water pump, fencing and other features around the square rely heavily on evidence such as Elias Vogler's watercolor painting, above.

If Count Zinzendorf had had his way, Salem Square would have been circular in design. According to a diagram drawn in 1755 or 1756 (see page 24), the count envisioned the new town in the Wachovia Settlement as a circular town divided by eight avenues radiating outward from the center, which would hold an octagonal congregation house.

After Zinzendorf's death in 1760, the more practical brethren charged with designing and building Salem chose to lay out their town on a conventional grid with an open town square, similar to other Moravian towns. The square was first planned to straddle Main Street, but was moved to the east as we see it today. The central square not only enhanced the beauty of the town, but was used for a number of public functions. The Moravians also clustered the church and various institutional buildings around the square, joining it by a long avenue to the graveyard, God's Acre.

With that plan in mind, the congregation leaders disagreed at first about where to situate their town square. They chose a site in 1766, planted a hundred and fifty fruit trees there, and built the first houses in Salem alongside it. Surveyor Christian Reuter's growing concern about an adequate water source ultimately shaped the 1768 decision to move the square to its present location, south of the original site. Here, Reuter believed, the elevation was low enough to ensure that two nearby springs would more effectively feed the cisterns on the square that would supply the community with water. On March 18, 1769, numerous sycamores and a few linden and catalpa trees were planted around the square, with a circle of eight cedar trees planted in the very center.

Salem Square now reflects a variety of early landscape features, including a circle of cedar trees and other trees mentioned in the records as early as 1769.

In 1772, Brother Matthew Miksch was granted permission to farm the square to augment his income. The square was soon fenced with post and clapboard to protect his crops against the cattle that often wandered through the town streets. When he gave up farming on the square in 1775, it was planted in grass, and sheep were kept within the fence to graze in the meadow. Brother Reuter persuaded the congregation to surround each tree with tree protectors beginning in 1777, a practice that continued for many years.

In 1804, the Market-Fire House was completed on the square. A stone corpse house was built on the east side of the square, and remained in use until early in the nineteenth century. It was used to store bodies until burial, and there the gravedigger also stored picks, shovels, and biers (including a special bier for children's funerals).

On the southwest corner, a large public cistern and a handpump were built for community use. These have been reconstructed in recent years.

From time to time, decisions had to be made about fencing in the square, or adding turnstyles to keep out cattle, or even altering paths to be sure the Single Brothers and the Single Sisters did not meet accidentally—or clandestinely.

In the late nineteenth century, the square took on the look of a municipal

The Market-Fire House, originally built in 1803 and reconstructed in 1955.

park. The fences were removed, an iron fountain stood in the center, and cropped lawns and formal flower beds surrounded the tall trees. Beginning in the 1950s, the square was gradually restored to its original appearance.

In 1989, a tornado uprooted many beautiful old trees in Salem Square. Disaster was turned into advantage, however. After careful research, the square was replanted to look as it did around 1840, according to documentary sources and Elias Vogler's watercolor (opposite page, top) painted around that time. Today the square is frequented by visitors from around the world who stroll about, attend the occasional concerts, or participate in such special celebrations as the traditional Easter Sunrise Service. Salem College students often study in the square and children play there, surrounded by history, in the shade of the modern-day trees.

God's Acre

(Top)
A sense of peace pervades God's Acre, with its rows of neat grave markers on the gently rolling hillside.

(Bottom)
An early-twentieth-century view of the entrance to God's Acre.

In April of 1766, the Moravians selected a graceful hillside site for their burial ground and called it, in the Moravian tradition, *Gottes Acker,* or "God's Acre." The name meant to them not a precise measurement of ground, but consecrated land where members of the congregation, the chosen children of God, were laid to rest to await the resurrection. In 1771, the site was cleared and surrounded by a fence, and in June of that year, the first member of the congregation was buried there. He was Brother John Birkhead, a weaver and one of the Single Brothers chosen to begin the building of Salem.

At Salem, as in most Moravian settlements, the burial ground is organized in large squares devoted to certain choirs of the congregation. In one square, married men and widowers are buried; in another, married women and widows. Other squares are designated for single men, single women, girls, and boys.

In the earliest years, European American and African American Moravians were buried side by side in God's Acre, in keeping with the Moravian belief that while congregation members were predestined to perform certain earthly roles in life, all were spiritual equals. But early in the nineteenth century, as prevailing attitudes about racial integration influenced the Moravians, a separate graveyard for African Americans was established at the south end of Church Street, adjoining a Strangers' Graveyard. Still later, a second graveyard for African Americans was laid out to the east of God's Acre, next to the private Salem Cemetery.

In keeping with the Moravian belief in the democracy of death, almost all graves in God's Acre are marked with a simple stone bearing the name of the deceased person. Sometimes the birth and death dates are given, along with the place of origin. On later graves, it is not uncommon to find a line of scripture or other appropriate words etched on the mark-

ers. The gravestones of children are slightly smaller than those for adults. In God's Acre at Salem, the graves face east, toward the rising sun. There is an austere beauty in their simplicity and symmetry, and the visitor who pauses to read names and dates leaves God's Acre better acquainted with the men, women, and children who lived and died in Salem.

Today, God's Acre is reserved for members of the thirteen Moravian churches belonging to the Salem Congregation.

Thousands of people come to Salem each year for the Easter Sunrise Service, a tradition that began for the Moravians in a spontaneous worship service held on Easter morning in 1732 on Count Zinzendorf's estate in Herrnhut. The first sunrise service in Salem took place in 1772.

In the days before Easter, the burial stones are scoured, the lawns are groomed, and the cemetery is filled with fresh flowers. The celebration begins before dawn on Easter Sunday morning in front of Home Moravian Church, when a minister proclaims to the crowd that has gathered, "The Lord is risen!"

"The Lord is risen indeed!" the con-

gregation and guests respond.

After part of the Easter liturgy is read, the throng moves in quiet procession toward God's Acre, as the Moravian bands, scattered throughout Salem and the graveyard, play the ancient chorales. One band plays a line, and then another band answers. The vibrant sound of brass and woodwind instruments playing in counterpoint to each other echoes over the gentle slopes of the graveyard and drifts throughout Salem.

As the sun's first rays appear, the Easter Sunrise Service, one of the oldest Moravian liturgies, comes to an end.

*(Above)
Easter Sunrise
service in
Herrnhut, c.1760,
from a series of
engravings of
Moravian customs
by Johann Rudolph
Holzhalb.*

*(Left)
The grave marker
of Peter Oliver,
one of the last
African American
Moravians to be
buried in God's
Acre before the
practice was
changed in 1816.*

29

3. *Living and Working in Salem, 1772 to 1776*

"Br. Graff held the Singstunde, reminding the congregation that ten years ago the savior gave to the conferenz His approval of the spot where Salem now stands."

Salem Diary, February 14, 1775

Salem was a haven of order and civility in the Carolina wilderness, surviving despite the pioneer settlement's vulnerability to panthers and wolves, to interlopers and vandals, and to strange fevers, storms, droughts, and floods. Then as now, the square was the focal point of the town. To the east of the square on Church Street, where Main Hall now stands, stood the Gemein Haus, or Congregation House, which was the central administrative building and place of worship. It housed the minister and his family, as well as the Single Sisters and the Girls' School. All the other buildings in these early years stood on Main Street. Facing the Congregation House across the square on Main Street was the Single Brothers' House, with their workshop behind it on what is now called Academy Street. Farther down Academy Street the Single Brothers had laid out gardens and built a spring house, a brewery and distillery, and a slaughterhouse. To the north of the square on Main Street stood a few small, sturdy half-timbered houses that had housed the first builders in Salem (see Street Guide, pp. 99–100). The Community Store faced the square.

Other important businesses were deliberately placed on the outskirts of town. The tavern was located to the south in an effort to limit encounters between congregation members and outsiders coming to Salem on business. To reduce the danger of fire, the potter's workshop and the blacksmith's shop were situated to the north.

In Salem, as in other Moravian congregation towns, the community used a labor system similar to the medieval guilds. Town leaders carefully chose the trades and crafts needed to support the town, as well as the masters and apprentices to practice them.

The Board of Supervisors orchestrated the number of craftsmen who could work in any given craft. When necessary, they appealed to the church elders in Europe to help them recruit skilled workers. A letter written by Frederic Marshall to the Unity board in Herrnhut in 1786 illustrates the level of concern for maintaining the skilled trades in Salem:

"If a good shoemaker, a faithful, industrious linen-weaver, and a tailor who understands his business can be found for the Single Brothers House here, the diaconie of the Single Brethren will gladly pay the expenses of

their journey. They also need a cook and a housekeeper. . . . All other craftsmen must come at their expense, though all brotherly assistance would be given to them if notice is sent in advance. A clock-maker and silversmith could find work enough; a coppersmith and pewterer the same. It should be noted that the trade in buckskin breeches is not good, and there are enough already being made; tinware we also have enough of. A glazier and painter would not have enough to do as the cabinet-makers do that work here. We would be glad to have a book-binder, but at present he would not find work enough unless he had some other trade also, or was willing to work at anything needed. Elderly people, or married people with several children, should not be advised to come."

Such attention to demographics was essential if the finely calibrated economy of the town was to thrive.

The Single Brothers' enterprises served as the cornerstone of Salem's industry, but other town residents contributed in substantial ways as well. Independent craftsmen, usually Married Brothers, ran church-owned businesses such as the pottery and the tavern. Traugott Bagge supervised the Community Store, which traded Salem's goods far and wide. Mat-

Chicken caster, probably made by potter Rudolph Christ in the early nineteenth century. Earthenware with green glaze.

30

thew Miksch and his wife Martha set up a smaller shop in their house where they sold gingerbread, tobacco, candles, and the hardy plants they grew in their garden.

The Moravians exhibited an awesome ingenuity and a capacity for hard work. The word spread rapidly through the southeastern colonies that these German-speaking religious folk in Salem made uncommonly good pottery, tinware, and other essential goods that most colonists could not produce for themselves.

Producing and selling goods were not the only activities practiced in Salem. Trained professionals such as the doctor, the surveyor, the minister, and teachers of the Boys' and the Girls' Schools played an important role in daily life. Their skills, as much as the tradesmen's fine goods, drew outsiders to Salem.

Women's contributions to economic life were also crucial to Salem's success. The Single Sisters, who at this time lived in the Gemein Haus, ran a school for girls and a laundry and grew vegetables for sale and for their own use. Women had a say in daily affairs through the Married Sisters' and the Single Sisters' choirs. Life in the Single Sisters' House, built in 1786, is described in Chapter 5.

To augment the skills and talents of the members of the congregation, the Moravians hired laborers. They also depended on the work performed by free and enslaved Africans and African Americans. These workers joined the Moravians as coopers, carpenters, teamsters, farmers, brickmakers, potters, blacksmiths, stablehands, and domestic helpers. In the eighteenth century the church owned all slaves and saw that their labor supported the common good rather than personal gain.

Even though the Moravians considered their slaves legal property, the enslaved African Americans who became members of the church enjoyed certain advantages. They worshipped together with white Moravians. A few enslaved children attended Salem schools. Enslaved African Americans who were church members were less likely to be sold out of the congregation and separated from their families. Some, like Peter Oliver, were able to negotiate with the church to gain some guarantee of stability in their lives.

Although they lived with the physical isolation that was a fact of life in any wilderness settlement, the Moravians were building comfort, convenience, and beauty into daily life in Salem. Their lives were austere, yet not devoid of pleasure. Moderation was the key, and alcohol and tobacco could be enjoyed so long as decorum was maintained. Music was considered a necessity, not a luxury, and the town would spawn poets and painters and gifted artisans.

The Moravians believed that all segments of life presented opportunities to serve God—whether as a missionary, a potter, a teacher, a doctor, a blacksmith, a nurse, a laundress, a musician, a cooper, or a teamster. They practiced, as Moravians still do, a religion based on peace, service, outreach, and devotion to the common good.

In this chapter you will learn more about the trades in Salem, which are now practiced in the Shultz Shoemaker Shop, the Timothy Vogler Gunsmith Shop, the silversmith shop in the John Vogler House, and the Single Brothers' House. You will also see another view of Salem life in the Miksch House.

A View of Salem in North Carolina (detail), by Ludwig Gottfried von Redeken, 1788. This ink drawing shows how Salem developed as a compact, orderly town, set in the rolling hills of the Carolina piedmont.

The Single Brothers' Choir

The Single Brothers' House, restored to its 1786 appearance.

The Single Brothers in Salem ran a small commercial empire, from which a good share of profits went to the congregation. Like the married tradesmen, who had shops in or adjoining their homes, the Single Brothers produced goods to be purchased by the congregation town. They also supplied the ever-growing procession of farmers, traders, and strangers who depended on Salem as a commercial center. At first they practiced their trades in the original Single Brothers' House itself. They soon needed more room, however, and in 1771 they built the Single Brothers' Workshop to create more additional space.

The Brothers lived in the Single Brothers' House, held meetings and religious services there, and took their meals there. Some worked there as well, while others worked in outbuildings such as the woodshed, the wash house, or the wagon shed. In 1786 an addition doubled the space of the Single Brothers' House, providing more room for workshops and living quarters. The cutaway view of the Single Brothers' House on pages 34–35 shows the activities that may have taken place there in 1786.

The hardworking Single Brothers also operated several large enterprises that were essential to the success of the town: the brewery and distillery, and the slaughterhouse. They were responsible for the springhouse that provided refrigeration and contained the early water source. They also ran a large plantation, or farm, where they grew food and essential crops.

LEARNING A TRADE

The Single Brothers' House was home to most Salem boys from the age of fourteen, when preparation for adult life began in earnest. Boys who showed intellectual promise were sent to a Moravian boarding school in Nazareth, Pennsylvania, to begin training as ministers, teachers, lawyers, merchants, or other leaders of the congregation.

Most boys, however, moved into the Single Brothers' House, where they followed the traditional apprenticeship system practiced in Europe for centuries. According to what the church elders and the boys' parents or guardians thought best, they were apprenticed to master craftsmen in the town. For the next few years, the boys worked hard under the direction and control of their masters, who now had more authority over the boys than their parents. The congregation was reminded, for instance, that "without the masters' consent parents should not give their sons money for the purchase of clothing. Parents and masters shall be admonished not to allow the boys to dress above their station, but modestly, lest they acquire an early taste for pride of clothing."

Once an apprenticeship was completed, the Single Brother went to work as a journeyman—a term traditionally used to denote a trained artisan who worked in different shops, advancing his skills. In Salem, however, the journeymen continued to live in the Single Brothers' House and to work for the master craftsmen there. A young man needed the permission of the church to set up shop on his own.

A SINGLE BROTHER SEEKS A WIFE

Only when a Brother had learned a trade and become self-supporting could he be eligible for marriage. The Lot, not love and romance, governed decisions about marriage in Salem. Congregation rules dictated that the Single Brothers and the Single Sisters have very little unsupervised contact with each other. The Moravian Church had stringent rules about marrying within the faith, and then only with the approval of the Lot. In addition, men with important positions were expected to be married.

When the Moravian elders suggested a marriage, or when a Single Brother requested permission to marry a certain Sister, the Lot was consulted and the reading of the Lot determined the outcome. No marriage could go forward without the Lot's approval, and no Sister was compelled to marry against her will, no matter what the Lot said.

Sometimes when a man wanted to marry, he decided on a possible bride and then submitted his request to church officials. They submitted the proposal to the woman in question; if she consented, the question was put to the Lot. If the prospective husband knew he wanted to marry but had no one in mind, an appropriate bride was suggested by church leaders. On rare occasions, the man and woman would then be introduced, if circumstances permitted. After their meeting, if the woman consented to the marriage, the matter was then submitted to the Lot.

The decision was in God's hands, the prospective couple would be reminded. If an affirmative Lot was drawn, the couple was officially betrothed, and the marriage

took place very quickly. Moravian marriages endured, many of them happily. Husband and wife were partners in marriage and often in their work as well.

Enslaved African Americans who were Moravians were encouraged to marry, despite colonial laws prohibiting slave marriages. Like other Moravian men, an African American man could submit a request to marry. While a European Moravian male's choice for a wife was subject to the Lot, more often than not this question was not submitted to the Lot for people of African descent because choices of a spouse were very limited. In either instance, women had the option to refuse an approved offer of marriage.

Perhaps one of the most-married Moravians was Anna Catharina Antes Kalberlahn Reuter Heinzmann Ernst, who was married and widowed four times. Her second husband was the surveyor Christian Gottlieb Reuter. The most persistent prospective bridegroom was the silversmith John Vogler. Between 1814 and 1819, he suggested seven possible brides (one twice), only to be greeted with eight negative Lots. Finally, in 1819, after Salem stopped using the Lot to arrange marriages for lay people, John Vogler asked Christina Spach, his second choice, to marry him, and she agreed.

After a Single Brother married, he moved away from the Single Brothers' House. He set up business in his home, or in a separate workshop, where he practiced his craft or trade. If this would generate competition harmful to his master or others, the brother would be directed to another way of earning his living.

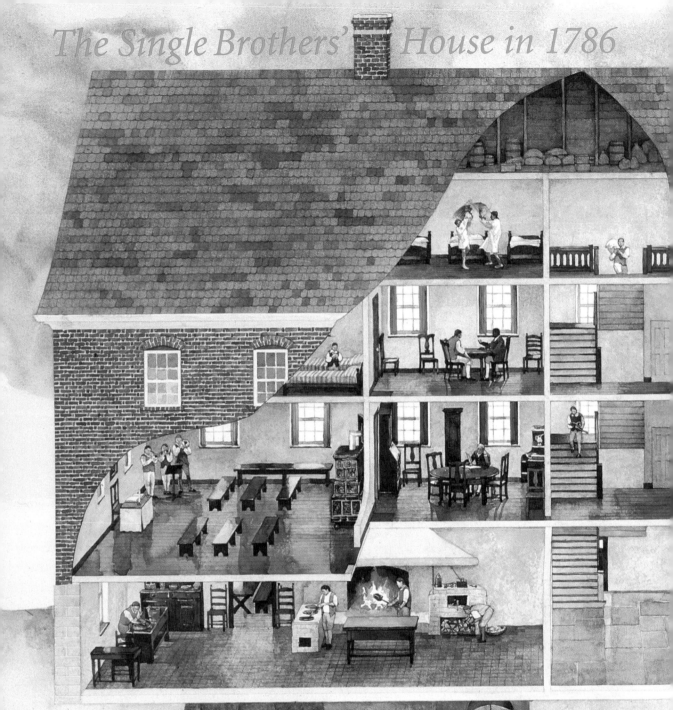

34

In 1786, the addition to their house completed, the Single Brothers now had twice the space they had before. This morning, nearly everyone has begun his tasks for the day. In the old, half-timbered section of the building, the artisans ply their trades: on the second floor, the joiner, tailor, and shoemaker, and on the ground floor, the weavers and the blue dyer, who uses the big vats of the original kitchen for his mixture of indigo.

The spacious new kitchen on the ground floor, with its spit, cook pots, and oven, makes it easier for the cooks to feed more than sixty Single Brothers. They need to keep ample supplies of food on hand, as well. The upper attic and the vaulted cellar below the kitchen are filled

with smoked meats, dried fruits and vegetables, beer, and sacks and barrels of grain.

One floor above the kitchen is the Saal. Next to it is the office of the Vorsteher, or business manager. In the evenings and on special days, the Saal is used for prayer services. This morning, however, some young apprentices are practicing their trombones—but not very well, judging by the look on the Vorsteher's face! How can he manage the affairs of the Single Brothers' Choir with such a commotion in the next room? And look! One of the apprentices is just now coming down the stairs, late again!

The floors above are devoted to dormitories and to sitting rooms, where groups of men and boys meet to study and converse. Peter Oliver, one of a very few African Americans who were members of the Single Brothers' Choir, is studying with one of the leaders of the choir to prepare for his baptism into the Moravian Church. But what is going on in the sleeping room above him?

Every inch of the Single Brothers' House is filled with activity, each man and boy applying his unique talents toward a common goal. The expansion of the Single Brothers' House reflects Salem's success.

"It is suggested that [John Dixon] be taken into the garden as assistant to Br. Priem. That would give Br. Priem time to look after the Brothers' kitchen, and bring things there into better order."

Minutes of the Salem Board, May 31, 1786

The Single Brothers' Choir

(Above)
The Vorsteher worked and slept in this room, which now features furniture made in Salem and Bethabara.

(Right)
The Saal organ is one of five organs in use in Wachovia by 1800.

THE SAAL, OR MEETING HALL

On the left as you enter the Single Brothers' House is the Saal, part of the 1786 addition to the house. This spacious room runs the depth of the building. Here the Brothers would congregate at the end of the day's work for Bible reading, singing, and prayer. The Saal was home to meetings, music rehearsals, lovefeasts, and other special worship services. The annual Single Brothers' choir festival, when boys were received into the choir, was held here, celebrated with a lovefeast.

The Saal is typical of early Moravian worship halls in its simplicity. Trappings were not important; only words and music mattered. Preachers and elders would read from the German Bible. Hymns were first sung to the accompaniment of brass ensembles, and later to the rich sounds of a pipe organ brought from Bethabara in 1798.

The small one-manual organ you see now was built for the Salem Gemein Haus in 1797–98 by organ builder David Tannenberg, a Moravian and the first American-trained organ builder. The organ's keys are capped in reverse, with ivory sharps and flats and ebony naturals. It has tin and wood pipes, and its pine case is painted to resemble mahogany wood-graining.

The organ in the Single Brothers' House was dismantled in the mid-nineteenth century and stored for over a hundred years. Thanks to the restoration completed in the 1960s and a restoration scheduled for 2006, the organ's beautiful sound endures.

THE VORSTEHER'S ROOM

At the rear of the main entrance hall is the room where the Single Brother's *Vorsteher*, or business manager, lived and had his office. The furnishings are not original to the room, although they are mostly Moravian-made, from the late eighteenth to early nineteenth centuries. The handsome desk-and-bookcase was created by Single Brother Johannes Krause, who resided in the Salem Single Brothers' House all of his working life. Brother Krause was a master joiner whose refined skill can be seen in the crotch cherry veneer with walnut banding and cherry crossbanding on this desk-and-bookcase.

THE KITCHEN

Downstairs, the 1786 kitchen has a large hooded fireplace, ovens, and sunken cooking pots that were heated by a flue from the hearth. The dining room, with its rows of plain tables, could have easily held the sixty-two boys and men who inhabited the Single Brothers' House and Workshop.

The trades demonstrated in the Single Brothers' House include those actually practiced there and those carried out at other locations—as well as some jobs that were not the responsibility of the Single Brothers, such as making pottery. The tradesmen who now work in the shops use tools and techniques unique to eighteenth-century Salem, reflecting the Moravians' Germanic roots and the style of their crafts and products.

The Trade Shops

(Above)
Weaving on an eighteenth-century loom.

(Top left)
The blue dyer tests wool being dyed in indigo.

(Left)
The tailor at work.

THE BLUE DYER'S SHOP

Until Matthew Weiss came from Bethlehem to establish a dyehouse in April 1774, cloth was dyed at home or sent away to Pennsylvania. Brother Weiss's tenure as the first dyer in Salem was short-lived, however. His behavior so offended the Brethren that he was expelled from Salem the next year; he eventually returned to Pennsylvania.

Sometime between 1786 and 1803, the old kitchen in the Single Brothers' House was turned into a dye shop. The blue dyer used indigo, a plant grown in South Carolina, to dye yarns and fabrics blue. Indigo is a difficult dye to use; it requires experience and skill to achieve consistent results. Other colors could be created in smaller quantities at home, using readily available materials. For example, walnut hulls yielded brown; onion skins produced yellow.

THE WEAVER'S ROOM

Because weaving was an essential craft, one of the first workers chosen to live in Salem in 1766 was the weaver Gottfried Praetzel. Initially Brother Praetzel set up his loom in the First House. After the Single Brothers' House was built, he moved there. He may have used a counterbalance loom similar to the ones in the weaver's room today. While this loom produces relatively simple weaves, a master weaver such as Brother Praetzel could have created interesting and varied patterns.

As time passed and the needs of the community grew, the Single Sisters also established a successful weaving business.

THE TAILOR'S SHOP

Men's garments in Salem were made by the tailor. In this shop you can see the cutting tools, bolts of cloth, and tailoring materials he would have used. He had the difficult challenge of pleasing customers who wanted the latest fashion, while at the same time he tried to abide by the guidelines laid out by the Moravian elders.

At times there was more work than the tailor in the Single Brothers' House could manage. In 1796, for instance, Sister Buttner, a widow, was "doing tailoring for the men." She had so much work that she asked permission "for a girl to learn from her." The Board of Supervisors cautioned her that "she should take only so much work as she can do herself."

In 1800, Gottlob Schroeter, who was Salem's master tailor, was assigned some Sisters to assist him with the sewing. In April of 1802, the Board of Supervisors approved a plan for Brother Schroeter to "ring the [town] bell for stopping work when it is too dark to thread a needle."

"Br. Schroeter complains that the Sisters are doing too much tailoring, which is injuring his trade. He can help the matter by doing his work as well as he can, so that no fault can be found with him."

Salem Board Minutes, June 11, 1808

37

The Trade Shops

Pouring pewter into a mold to make a spoon. As they come out of the mold, the hot spoons are dropped in a basket; they are later trimmed and polished.

Examples of the Salem tinsmith's craft: a decorative cake pan, a hand churn, and a sausage stuffer (all 19th century).

THE TIN AND PEWTER SHOP

The Single Brothers did not work with tin and pewter, but other tradesmen in Salem did. In this shop, you can see the types of tin and pewter products that were made in Salem, as well as the tools that produced them. Old Salem has the largest collection of early pewter molds used by one family in the United States.

Three generations of this family, Johann Christoph Reich, his sons John Philip and Friedrich Jacob, and his grandson William Augustus Reich, were sheet metal workers in Salem. They used hammer and anvil to shape sheets of tin, copper, and tin-coated iron into buckets, stills, candleholders, candle molds, sausage stuffers, funnels, cookie cutters, tin boxes, pots and pans, and pipes. They molded spoons, plates, and bowls out of pewter. And as the Reich House on Church Street illustrates today, they worked copper into window muntins and downspouts.

Today Old Salem tradesmen work with reproduction tools and molds to reproduce the items the Reich family made early in the nineteenth century. The shop is located in what was identified as the weaver's room in Frederic Marshall's 1769 plan of the Single Brothers' House.

Peter Oliver

Peter Oliver, a potter, was born into slavery in Virginia in 1766. He was one of a few African American men to become members of the Single Brothers' Choir and live in the Single Brothers' House.

Little is known of his childhood except that he was named Oliver. At the age of eighteen he was leased by his Virginia owner to Michael Ranke of Bethania. When his lease was about to expire, Oliver asked the Moravians to buy him. Perhaps he realized that if he could not be free, life with the Moravians would be better than with another master.

In 1785 his lease was taken over by the Single Brothers in Salem, and in February 1786 Frederic Marshall purchased him for the church for $100. Oliver prepared to join the Salem congregation by studying the Bible, and learning to read and write. On November 12, 1786, he was baptized as Peter Oliver and became a member of the Single Brothers' Choir.

Brother Oliver moved to Bethabara to work for master potter Rudolph Christ in January 1788. When Christ moved to Salem to run the pottery there, Oliver was purchased by the new Bethabara potter, Gottlob Krause, to be his assistant. Alarmed that Krause might sell him arbitrarily, Oliver negotiated a bond with the church guaranteeing that he would not be sold so long as he conducted himself according to church principles.

Although no confirming documents have been found, a memoir about Brother Oliver suggests he had earned enough money by 1801 to purchase his freedom. In Febrary 1802 he married Christina Bass, a free mulatto woman, and they settled on a farm near Salem. They had six children, but three sons died in infancy.

Peter Oliver died in 1810, at the age of forty-four. His association with the Moravian Church gave him some advantages shared by few of his race. He could read and write; while a slave he secured a bond that he would not be sold; and he purchased his freedom. He was buried in God's Acre, one of the last African American Moravians to be buried there.

Gottfried Aust

Brother Gottfried Aust was born April 5, 1722, in Silesia. The son of a linen weaver, Aust moved to Herrnhut when he was nineteen and became a potter's apprentice. He traveled to Bethlehem, Pennsylvania, in 1754, and moved to Bethabara in October 1755.

For sixteen years, Brother Aust ran the Bethabara pottery, producing a wide range of utilitarian housewares—bowls and basins, plates and porringers, chamber pots and flower pots, roasting pans, tea pots, and clay pipes. He became Salem's master potter in 1771. Irascible, opinionated, and often difficult to get along with, Aust was a hard taskmaster, in perennial conflict with his young apprentices. Despite these traits, he was an outstanding craftsman.

Aust's mastery of traditional Germanic pottery designs was enhanced in the early 1770s when an English potter arrived in Salem and taught him the secrets of making Queensware (also called creamware, a fine, high-fired cream-colored earthenware which was refined by Wedgwood and other master craftsmen in England). Brother Aust had already produced ceramic pottery reminiscent of Queensware, but the encounter with this anonymous potter and the English pottery worker William Ellis led to the production of more sophisticated ceramic pottery.

By 1786 Brother Aust was nearly bedridden with cancer, and in 1788 he traveled to Pennsylvania for treatment. He died in Lititz, Pennsylvania, on October 28, 1788, leaving behind his third wife, a bequest of fifty pounds to help purchase a town clock for Salem, and his legacy as the first of Salem's master potters.

THE POTTER'S SHOP

The fame of Salem pottery quickly spread through the Carolinas. There was such demand for the Moravians' durable, attractive pottery that pottery-making became the largest commercial enterprise in town. Run by the congregation, not the Single Brothers, the potter's shop was located two blocks to the north of the Single Brothers' House.

Salem potters produced a wide variety of tableware and storage jars turned on a wheel, molded bottles and pipes, and molded Queensware. They experimented with techniques such as tin-glazing (faience), which was rare in America at that time. They also manufactured the colorful tile stoves seen in several Old Salem buildings, including the Single Brothers' House and the Miksch House.

In the replica of a potter's shop in the Single Brothers' House, you can see a glaze mill, a pipe mold, and a potter's wheel used by Salem's second master potter, Rudolph Christ (1750–1833). In the Boys' School (see p. 66) there is a complete exhibit of Salem pottery.

(Left) Large earthenware plate made by Gottfried Aust in 1773. It was used as a trade sign for the pottery shop.

Examples of decorated pottery plates, a storage jar, and a decorative inkstand made in Salem.

(Above)
The joiner works with the same tools an artisan would have used in the eighteenth and early nineteenth centuries.

(Right)
A turner working at a springpole lathe.

THE JOINER'S SHOP

The Single Brothers operated a large woodworking shop in a building behind the Single Brothers' House. This shop served the community until the Brothers' House was closed early in the nineteenth century. Salem's joiners were versatile: they had to be both skilled carpenters and talented cabinetmakers. They fashioned tables, chairs, shelves, desks, and case goods, as well as window sashes and doors.

Moravian furniture reflected its Germanic origins in its massive proportions, simplicity of form, and solid construction. While function was the cabinetmaker's prime concern, he made his products beautiful as well, with elaborate moldings, finely grained woods, and turned or carved details.

In today's shop, you will see tradesmen reproducing early Moravian furniture and making items to be used in the museum. They work in the style of the early Moravian craftsmen, using tools and equipment that are identical to what would have been used in the late eighteenth and early nineteenth centuries.

THE TURNER'S SHOP

The turner used a lathe to shape legs and spindles for chairs and tables, knobs for furniture, spinning wheels, and many other objects, both decorative and useful. While the lathe spun a rough cylinder of wood on its axis, the turner carved the wood with a sharp turning tool.

In the early years in Salem, turning was usually done by joiners and cabinetmakers. The turner Karsten Petersen eventually became one of Salem's best-known cabinetmakers. In 1806 he was brought to the New World to work as a missionary with the Creek Nation in Georgia, where he trained the Native Americans to make spinning wheels and looms. When he returned to Salem in 1813, he set up shop in the former slaughterhouse and began to produce spinning wheels and other tools for spinners and weavers, as well as furniture with turned legs and architectural turnings such as balusters for stair rails.

The lathe used in the Single Brothers' House is a replica of an eighteenth-century springpole lathe. The turner operated it by pushing a pedal attached to a cord wound about the work being turned, causing it to spin on its axis. A wooden spring, the springpole, kept wood in motion by returning the pedal after every stroke.

Architecture Key

The Single Brothers' House

600 South Main Street. Built in 1769 with an addition in 1786; restored 1961. Lot 62

Designed by Frederic William Marshall, the Single Brothers' House was originally planned to be the size you see now, but it was built in two stages.

The northern section was built in 1769 in *fachwerk*—half-timbered framing filled in with brick. The clay-based mortar the Moravians made was not stable enough to use in solid brick walls, so they used the half-timbering technique they were familiar with from Germany.

In 1786, the Moravians built an addition to the Single Brothers' House with solid brick walls, using strong lime-based mortar. The addition had the same proportions as the original section, with new features such as elliptical relieving arches over the windows and doors.

The building as you now see it has been restored to its 1786 appearance. Over the years, the pent roof was removed and the fachwerk section of the building was covered with stucco, and later with weatherboards. This covering remained in place until the building was restored in 1964. Old Salem relied on Marshall's original building plans for determining how to restore features such as the pent roof.

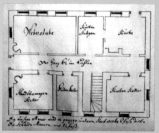

Frederic William Marshall's design for the Single Brothers' House in 1769.

Several roofing features show how the builder tried to protect the walls from water damage. The main roof had a kick eave, formed by a wedge of wood under the shingles at the roof's edge. The kick eave can be seen in many examples of early Moravian architecture. Raising the angle of the roof line at the eave sent falling rainwater farther away from the foundation.

The framing elements were marked with two sets of marks. The Roman numeral indicated a timber's placement from right to left. The timbers for each side of the building were marked with a different symbol after the Roman numeral, in this case a slash.

Halfway down the facade, a pent roof, built out from the facade and covered with wood shingles, protected the lower half of the walls.

The Miksch House

This small yellow house was the first in Salem to be occupied by a single family, Matthew and Henrietta Miksch and their daughter Martha. They moved to Salem in 1771.

"Br. Thomas Buttner has a mind to undertake the bakery . . . He wishes permission to bake gingerbread, but for many years this has been the chief source of income for Br. and Sr. Miksch, so that cannot be changed now."

Salem Minutes, October 29, 1799

When Maria Christina Henrietta Petermann married Johann Matthaeus Miksch in 1764, two pioneering Moravian families were joined together. Henrietta was born in 1733 in Wetteravia, near Herrnhaag. She was brought up in a Moravian congregation school and was received into the Herrnhaag congregation when she was fourteen.

She lived in London for three years, where she learned to speak English. In 1751 she traveled to North America with Bishop Spangenberg and other congregation members. For thirteen years Henrietta lived in Bethlehem, Pennsylvania, first teaching in the girls' school there and later serving as the leader of the Single Sisters' Choir.

Matthaeus, or Matthew, was the son of Moravian missionaries to St. Croix, Virgin Islands. When his father died there, Matthew's mother Martha Elisabeth Jahn Miksch married Bishop Spangenberg, and Matthew came to know his stepfather far better than he had ever known his father. As an apprentice he learned bookbinding, but when he moved to Herrnhaag in September 1748, there was no work in his craft. Therefore, he was employed making leather goods.

Matthew was called to Bethlehem, Pennsylvania, in 1754. After doing missionary work among the Native Americans in New York and serving as treasurer of the Single Brothers' Choir, he was called to Wachovia in 1764. That year, when he was thirty-three and she thirty,

Matthew and Henrietta married and moved to Bethabara, where they operated the community store. It was a shared responsibility. While Matthew was ill for a year, Henrietta ran the store on her own. Their marriage was blessed with three children, but only one, Martha Elizabeth, survived to adulthood.

In 1769 Traugott Bagge came to Bethabara and was put in charge of the Bethabara Store. Brother Miksch served as storekeeper under Brother Bagge's supervision for two years before he and his family moved to Salem in 1771.

BROTHER AND SISTER MIKSCH LOOK FOR WORK

Brother Miksch did not know how he would support himself and his family in Salem, but the Board of Supervisors helped him to find a solution. In March 1772, the board granted him permission to open a small shop; in April it was suggested that he might piece together a living by "selling candles, shaving, making snuff and fine-cut tobacco, selling oil and whale oil, growing young fruit trees, selling garden seeds, cabbage, pickled cucumbers, turnips, dried fruit and the like." The elders predicted correctly that this would be a difficult way to earn a livelihood. Matthew was also granted permission in 1772 to farm the open land of Salem Square, which he did until 1775.

Brother and Sister Miksch were hard workers and equal partners in their business ventures. By 1775 they had hit their stride. They sold gingerbread and candles made by Sister Miksch. Brother Miksch grew hardy plants in the garden and processed tobacco, which he worked into large twists for smoking and small twists for chewing. Eventually, he produced snuff that was bottled in small jars made in the Salem pottery. He also began to travel now and then to Cross Creek (now Fayetteville) to sell tallow, tobacco products, and candles.

In 1785, because the Single Brothers were running the town's only bakery, the Single Sisters had to enter their shop to buy bread. The Moravians did not want single men and women to mingle unchaperoned, and the Board of Supervisors felt it would be better for the Single Sisters to

Architecture Key

The Miksch House

532 South Main Street. Built 1771; restored 1960. Lot 59

Unlike the brick and half-timbered construction of the other early houses in Salem, the Miksch House was built of sturdy, carefully dovetailed logs, probably because logs were the most accessible building material. The church planners, however, had decreed that the main street of their new congregation town would not be defaced by plain log houses. After all, this was to be a cosmopolitan trading center, not a rough pioneer settlement. Therefore, the log structure was soon encased in clapboard and painted yellow.

Like Salem's first houses, the Miksch House was designed with a central chimney that served multiple rooms. This house is somewhat smaller than the others, though, and at first had only a small entry and two rooms. While the Miksches lived there, a lean-to addition at the back was built on and a room in the second-floor loft was finished, giving the house the configuration we see today.

With the passage of time, the Miksch house was absorbed into a larger building and hidden by the addition of lean-tos, false fronts, and dormer windows. Fortunately, the shell of the house survived many of these changes so that with careful architectural and archaeological analysis, and help from documentary sources, the building could be restored accurately.

The Miksch house absorbed into the urban Winston-Salem landscape in the 1950s, above, and, opposite page, restored to its 1785 exterior appearance. The log tobacco shed, left, replaces the shed where Matthew would have processed the tobacco he grew.

Both the Miksch tobacco shed and the house feature tile roofs. Tile was a favored roofing material in the eighteenth century because it was fireproof.

The dovetailing of the logs on the Miksch tobacco shed, a reconstruction of the outbuilding as it was probably built in 1782 or 1783. The squared timbers are very similar to the log construction of the Miksch house, now hidden under clapboard.

The Miksch House

*(Right)
Henrietta Miksch
cooked all the
family's meals in
this fireplace. The
best room, which
served as living
room and shop
space, is seen
through the
doorway.*

*"Br. and Sr. Misch
can no longer spare
their daughter
Martha Ealizabeth
from their home,
and Sr. A. Benigna
Benzien will take
her place as teacher
in the girls school."*

*Salem Minutes,
October 25, 1790*

*Ceramic tile stove
now in the Miksch
House, made in
Salem in the late
eighteenth century.*

purchase bread from a married couple. Therefore, the board asked the Miksch family to sell the Single Brothers' baked goods to townspeople and outsiders.

Sister Miksch, practical business-woman that she was, quite naturally promoted her own baked goods over the Single Brothers' bread. Just as naturally, the town elders scolded her for doing so. In the 1790s, the Miksch family earned most of their income baking and selling ginger-bread, and making and selling candles.

Over the years, Brother Miksch performed a variety of special services for the congregation. He helped to settle estates and rode to Salisbury on court matters. He also assisted Brother Reuter, the surveyor, in surveying the line between Rowan and Surry counties. In the 1790s, Brother Miksch was appointed forester of the congregation. Brother Reuter had carefully managed the forest of Wachovia as an essential resource. Unfortunately, Brother Miksch allowed people to cut too much wood. The Salem Board warned him repeatedly about the dangers of ruining the forest, and finally appointed Johann Leinbach to replace him in 1798.

Martha grew up working beside her parents in the house. She was a student at the girls' school and later, as a Single Sister, taught at the school herself. As her parents' business grew, they needed her to help them at home, and she was replaced by another teacher.

Martha no doubt brought joy and comfort to her parents, especially in their old age. In 1792 she married Samuel Benjamin Vierling, the town physician. She raised her stepdaughter and gave birth to five daughters and three sons of her own. Brother and Sister Miksch must have taken great pleasure in their grandchildren, who lived just up the hill on Church Street.

By 1805, both Matthew and Henrietta Miksch were aging and infirm, and the Vierlings took them into their home to care for them. Brother Miksch died in 1810, when he was 79, and the next year, Sister Miksch died at the age of 77.

LIVING IN THE MIKSCH HOUSE

Life in this small, snug house was simple and busy. Because they did not have a special shop area, the Miksches served their customers from the living room. The goods they produced and sold would have been stored in the cellar or in the loft before it became Martha's bedroom. In the living room and kitchen you can see samples of the type of ginger cakes Henrietta baked and the tobacco products Matthew produced.

The house has been furnished with Moravian furniture from the period, pieces similar to those the family would have used: sturdy, practical, and well-made chairs, tables, and cupboards.

The iron jamb stove in the living room comes from an old house in Alamance County. With its Germanic heart and flower decoration, it is like the one that would have kept the two downstairs rooms warm. The colorful tile stove in the loft upstairs was made in Salem.

After the shed was built behind the house in 1782 or 1783, Matthew may have worked out there, drying and processing tobacco. He probably stored some of his goods there as well.

Gardens in Old Salem

Along Salt Street you will find a series of "family gardens," a term first used in Moravian records in 1775. The family gardens you see today along Salt Street have been carefully re-created to show the plants that would have been grown by the Moravians at various times in the eighteenth and early nineteenth centuries.

The Miksch House is a good example of how the Moravians used their long, narrow lots. The house was built on the street. Next to the house was a swept yard where the family would do laundry, prepare food, and work on other household chores. Behind the shed, the back half of the lot was laid out in two rows of neat garden beds, or "squares," with a long path between them.

The garden was first of all a source of food and home medical remedies. Families planted vegetables and fruits and herbs for both cooking and medicinal purposes all together. Many families also had "outlots," larger parcels of land on the outskirts of Salem, where they could keep livestock such as horses, cows, and pigs, and grow potatoes, corn, grain, and other field crops.

Restoration of the Single Brothers' Gardens is currently under way. The gardens, located behind the Single Brothers' House and Workshop, will restore the landscape to its early-nineteenth century appearance.

Although most of the houses on Main Street and Salt Street are now private residences, the gardens are open to the public.

The Miksch lot, with its sequence of house, swept yard, shed, and garden area with two rows of square beds.

The vegetables and flowers in Old Salem are heirloom plants, old varieties similar to those grown there in the early days.

Beans grow on the trellises in the Miksch garden.

While the gardens were utilitarian, they were also pleasing to the eye: flowers were planted with the vegetables and herbs in the squares and around the boundaries of the lots.

4. *Salem in the American Revolution*

"We Brethren do not bear arms, and we neither will do personal service in the army nor enlist others to do it; but we will not refuse to bear our share of the burdens of the land in these disturbed times if reasonable demands are made."

Declaration of the Single Brothers, May 22, 1778

"We and each of us will gladly serve the Public, whenever we can do it according to our Consciences; however [*sic*] beg leave to inform you, that taking Seats in the Committee is against our Consciences, as we do not carry Arms, and have had that Privilege granted us, previous to our settling here. We shall nevertheless be found at all time bearing due allegiance to our sovereign Lord king [*sic*] George the Third; to be Well-wishers & Promoters of the Welfare of the Province and county we live in, and never do any thing which shall hurt the country."

Traugott Bagge, addressing The Surry County Committee appointed August 11, 1775, to "meet and consult for our common peace liberty & safety."

Although the Revolutionary War was never fought on Wachovia soil, it affected the people of Salem in many ways. It challenged the Moravians' pacifist beliefs, which were a cornerstone of their faith. It also called into question their loyalty to the British government, which was founded on their good relationship with Lord Granville. In the face of the colonial government's demands that they take up arms and swear loyalty to the United States of America, the Moravians strongly maintained a neutral position.

Ironically, the war, not peacetime, turned Salem into the vital trading and commercial center it aspired to become. The Moravians were soon carrying heavy wartime responsibilities, producing food, pottery, woven cloth, leather goods, and other critical supplies and equipment for military and civilian needs. Strangers rode in and out of Salem in unprecedented numbers, seeking supplies, shelter, and medical care.

The quest for freedom took on another dimension in 1775 when enslaved Africans and African Americans in the southern colonies heard that Lord Dunmore, the royal governor of Virginia, had promised freedom to any slaves who fought for the British against the American rebels. That news inevitably reached the ears of the church-owned slave Sambo, who had worked for the Moravians in Salem for almost four years. Sambo ran away from Salem on July 2, 1775, but was captured and returned three weeks later.

After Great Britain closed key American ports in 1775, Salem merchant Traugott Bagge had the thankless task of enforcing higher prices in the Community Store. Brother Bagge became the virtual purchasing agent for the Continental troops in western North Carolina during the Revolutionary War. He and his fellow tradesmen provided supplies, from lead to sugar, coffee, tobacco, and salt. On a single day in 1776, Colonel Martin Armstrong ordered Salem, Bethabara, and Bethania to supply two thousand pounds of meat and enough cornmeal to feed two thousand men for eight days.

The Moravians played host to minute men and provisioned colonial militia in the area. Frequently the streets and shops of Salem teemed with strangers. Sometimes there were a hundred to be fed in a

North Carolina paper currency did not have the same value as coins, or "hard" money, but merchants such as Traugott Bagge were forced to accept it.

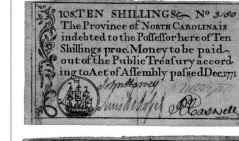

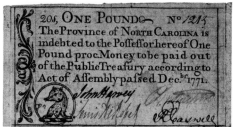

46

day and sixty to be lodged at night. Since the Salem congregation in 1776 numbered 105 adults and 22 children, the burden some days nearly doubled the population of the town.

Everyday activities such as educating Salem youngsters and tending the sick carried on as usual. As the war wore on, the people of Salem cared for many of the wounded soldiers from nearby battles and skirmishes. Most building projects in Salem came to a standstill. The Brethren did construct a municipal water works in 1778, possibly because wartime responsibilities made the daily task of procuring water more difficult.

The war curtailed the flow of letters from Pennsylvania and from Europe, cutting off the congregation from their regular communication with other Moravian communities. Brother and Sister Marshall had sailed for Europe on church business in 1775, but the war made it impossible for them to return to Salem. As their access to the larger world shrank, the Moravians turned more than ever to their religious faith for spiritual sustenance and for the strength to carry out the ongoing work of the congregation.

LOYALTY TO THE CAUSE

In August 1778, the North Carolina government published an order commanding citizens to swear allegiance to the new government, or abandon their property and depart within sixty days for Europe or the West Indies. This was pointedly directed at the Moravians and other religious groups such as the Quakers, the Dunkards, and the Mennonites whose religious beliefs forbade their bearing arms, and who voiced conscientious objection to swearing an oath of allegiance to the United States of America.

When the Moravians sent a petition to the North Carolina Assembly asking to be exempted from renouncing allegiance to the King, it was denied. Fortunately the Assembly must have feared that the productive Moravians would indeed follow their principles and emigrate, because soon afterward it passed a resolution postponing the deadline for taking the loyalty oath. Later, the Moravians signed a modified affirmation of loyalty,

which protected their land and property and ensured that they would not be forced to perform military duty.

THE WAR COMES CLOSER TO SALEM

In 1780 and 1781, the war was being fought in North Carolina, South Carolina, and Virginia. In August 1780, Bethabara, with 42 adults and 27 children in its congregation, was overrun by three hundred Virginia militia men, who camped in the town for three weeks. After the Battle of Kings Mountain in October, where Lord Cornwallis and his British troops were defeated, Bethabara hosted five hundred soldiers and three hundred prisoners for nineteen days. Some of the prisoners were sent to Salem.

In February 1781, Lord Cornwallis and his army marched through town, determined despite their defeat at Kings Mountain to conquer North Carolina. Several days later, nearly five hundred cavalry troops camped in Salem, throwing the town into chaos. As well as unruly soldiers, there were civilian families of men, women, and children who had placed themselves under the "protection"

(Above) The Battle of Guilford Courthouse, near Greensboro, here re-enacted by the North Carolina Fifth Militia, was the closest military engagement to Salem.

(Left) Hundreds of soldiers would camp outside Salem in tent cities like this one.

"The whole land cries for peace, and a more kindly administration of the laws."

Salem Diary, November 26, 1778

47

Salem in the American Revolution

On July 4, costumed interpreters often re-enact one of the first Independence Day celebrations in the country with a blessing, songs, and a dramatic torchlight procession around Salem Square.

"Resolved that the fourth Day of July be and is hereby appointed a day of General Thanksgiving and praise to Almighty God ."

Proclamation by North Carolina Governor Alexander Martin, May 16, 1783

of the British army. British soldiers stole from the store and from residences, even snatching the wash off the clothesline at one house.

American soldiers could be dangerous as well. When about a dozen of General Greene's men rode into town on February 16, they "lived at discretion in the town," the Salem Diary complained. They got drunk at the tavern and threatened the lives and homes of several Brothers and Sisters, including Brother Bagge, twice holding a pistol to his breast.

The Moravians never knew from day to day who might appear in the town, friend or foe, and what demands, reasonable or unreasonable, might be thrust upon them. They worried about the safety of their homes and their children.

At last in 1781, Lord Cornwallis surrendered, but peace did not come immediately. It was not until September 21, 1782, that King George III acknowledged that the American colonies were independent. On January 20, 1783, the Preliminary Treaty of Peace, signed in Paris, officially ended the Revolutionary War.

SALEM CELEBRATES INDEPENDENCE

North Carolina was the only state to declare a day of thanksgiving for the return of peace on July 4, 1783, and as far as can be told, the Moravians were the first people in North Carolina to honor the proclamation. The details of the first Independence Day celebration in the new country were faithfully recorded in the Salem Diary. Trombones greeted the day, which was filled with religious celebrations. At eight in the evening, the congregation assembled in the Gemein Haus Saal, where the choir sang "Praise be to Thee, Who sittest above the cherubim." Then, according to the Diary, "The congregation formed a circle in front of the Gemein Haus, and from there passed in procession through the main street of the town, with music and the antiphonal song of two choirs. The street was illuminated. Returning to the Gemein Haus the congregation again formed a circle, and with the blessing of the Lord was dismissed to rest. Hearts were filled with the peace of God, evident during the entire day and especially during the procession, and all around there was a silence, even the wind being still."

SETTLING INTO PEACETIME

Life slowly began to return to normal in Salem. Now, instead of the dangers of militia and marauders and British dragoons, the Salem Diary recorded the perils of measles, of fierce storms, of killing frosts, of panthers, wolves, and mad dogs. New building projects were planned, such as the long-awaited Single Sisters' House. On New Year's Eve, the Moravians welcomed the new year with a lovefeast and the music of trombones—the first year of peace in eight years.

The Salem Waterworks

Before the Revolution, the Moravians in Salem had planned to build a municipal waterworks system to provide a reliable water supply. In 1778 they finally built their waterworks, running water from the spring northwest of Salem through wooden pipes to five sites in the town. Salem was the first town in the Southeast to build a municipal water system.

Christian Reuter, the surveyor, had chosen the water source several years earlier, a site with two springs located about a mile to the northwest of town. Johannes Krause, a joiner, chose the route the pipes would follow and supervised the digging of the ditches and the laying of the pipes. Christian Triebel, a carpenter, cut and bored the pipes, shaped from oak and yellow-pine logs. The Single Brothers, aided by two German day laborers, dug the trench between Salem and the water source.

The water system was designed with five stations. The first was a standpipe on the corner of modern-day Bank and Main streets, near the first houses. The water then flowed to another pipe at the southwest corner of the square, opposite the Community Store. It was also pumped into the kitchens of the Single Brothers' House, the Tavern, and the Gemein Haus, where it flowed out of wooden spigots such as the one in the Single Brothers' House, right.

The Salem Waterworks system worked by gravity. The springs were at a higher elevation than the town, so that the water built up pressure as it flowed to the town. The flow of water could be plugged and shunted from one place to another, without pumps, and could "spring" for a few hours at a time.

As the town expanded, Salem outgrew the first waterworks, so that a second system was intalled in 1828, and a third in 1878.

(Left)
The spigot that provided water to the Single Brothers' House still functions today.

(Above)
The Community
Store, restored to its
1775 appearance.
Now called
T. Bagge: Merchant,
it is an Old Salem
museum shop.

(Right)
Counterfeit paper
currency that was
confiscated by
Brother Bagge,
who wrote on it,
"Counterfeit,
condemned by me.
Traugott Bagge."

produced in quantity, such as butter, tallow, wheat, and skins. He and his assistants would take wagonloads of goods to Charleston, Philadelphia, and the North Carolina ports of Cross Creek (Fayetteville), Wilmington, and New Bern.

Because Brother Bagge traveled so much on store business, he came to know the colonial landscape firsthand. His shrewd business sense, combined with his experiences outside Wachovia, helped him understand the events taking place in the outside world better than many of the Brethren. Bagge also came to be known and respected throughout North Carolina as a smart, honest businessman and a trusted citizen who took an active role in civic affairs beyond Salem.

During the war he represented Salem's interests in negotiations with the North Carolina government, neighboring communities, and the Continental and British armies. The outbreak of the war changed how he did business. He cut back his inventory to items that were most necessary, and tried to fill the large orders of the Continental Army. In 1775, he stopped selling tea in the store to avoid criticism from outsiders that the Moravians were loyalists.

When North Carolina's Provincial Congress mandated the issue of paper money, it caused more problems for Brother Bagge and other businesses. Paper money did not have the worth of the "hard" money it replaced, but if shop owners or artisans criticized or refused paper money, they lost their right to do business and were considered traitors. Counterfeiters quickly set to work circulating worthless paper notes (left), which vigilant shopkeepers tried to spot and confiscate.

In 1782 Brother Bagge was elected to the North Carolina Assembly. Although Moravians usually did not get involved in political affairs, he accepted this office because he hoped he could "help to check the wasting and plundering going on in the land, and also that I might help to establish the rights of the Unity in Wachovia." He was appointed a commissioner for his district of North Carolina, as well as a justice of the peace for the county. He died on April 1, 1800, and was buried in God's Acre.

Traugott Bagge, the proprietor of the Salem Community Store, played a central role in helping Salem maintain its neutrality and endure the hardships imposed by the American Revolution. He was born in 1729 in Gothenburg, Sweden. In 1767, when he was thirty-eight years old, Brother Traugott Bagge was called to Wachovia with his wife, Rachel Nickelson. From Bethabara, Brother Bagge moved to Salem in 1772 to oversee all the trade and commerce flowing in and out of the town.

The Community Store offered nearly all the necessities—and the rare luxuries—that could not be grown, manufactured, or improvised in Salem itself. These included foodstuffs such as coffee, tea, sugar, salt, rice, chocolate, and spices. The store also carried tools and supplies that the town's craftsmen needed, such as whetstones, paint brushes, and indigo. Other items listed in the store's account books were buttons, ribbons, buckles, flannel and calico, curtain rings, pins and needles, window glass, curry combs, blankets, violin strings, and stirrups. To obtain these goods Brother Bagge sold or traded commodities that the Moravians

Architecture Key

T. Bagge: Merchant

626 South Main Street. Built 1775; restored 1954. Lot 63.

In 1775 the Community Store moved from the Two-Story, or Second, House to the permanent store building opposite Salem Square.

It was the first structure in Salem to be built entirely of masonry. The walls were constructed of stone rubble laid up with red clay mortar, which was then covered with a form of stucco. Masons scored the stucco with grooves to simulate the outlines of cut stone. Despite the fact that the wartime economy made it scarce and expensive, lime mortar was used to fill in the grooves. Other structures with similar stucco walls are the Bagge House, diagonally across the street from the store, the Boys' School, the Winkler Bakery, and the Single Brothers' House 1786 foundation.

The main floor of the store was the selling area, and the cellars were used for storage. The south entrance led to the Bagges' living quarters, where Brother and Sister Bagge lived with their daughter Anne Elizabeth and twin sons, Charles and Frederic.

In 1837 a brick second story was added (see 1895 photograph, top). The building functioned as a store and residence until 1907. After another exterior renovation, it was used solely as a residence. In 1954 the Community Store was restored, using evidence such as the Von Redeken drawing (right).

The store building in 1895.

Ludwig von Redeken's 1788 View of Salem documents the original roofline and appearance of the community store, shown here on the square, at the bottom right.

The Bagge House, diagonally across the street from the store, was originally built by Traugott Bagge for his assistant, George Biwighausen. Destroyed in the late nineteenth century, it was rebuilt in 1970 and is now a private residence.

The walls of the Community Store have grooves filled with lime to simulate the look of cut stone walls.

5. *After the American Revolution to 1800*

Like Americans everywhere, the Moravians paid a great price for the long struggle for political independence. Repercussions from the war affected almost every aspect of daily life in Salem. Whether the Moravians liked it or not, the war had brought the outside world to Salem. The countless strangers who came into town exposed the Moravians to new ideas and new ways. In addition, the war forced them to look outward, interacting with their neighbors and taking a stand on important issues affecting the emerging nation.

The Moravians in Salem had maintained a vital business center during the Revolution, and on that foundation they began to build a new prosperity. By the end of 1783, the town was turning a modest profit, partly because stores in nearby towns had been unable to reopen. That year, Traugott Bagge had made a dangerous trip to Charleston to replenish the supplies exhausted by the demands of two armies. Soon the Salem town store was fully stocked and bustling with more customers than ever.

Building projects that had been postponed because of the war now took priority. The Single Sisters' House was the first on the list, but when the Salem Tavern burned down in 1784, the Single Sisters were told that rebuilding the tavern had to come first. The building materials that had been reserved for the Single Sisters' House were used for the new tavern. It would be made of brick rather than the half-timbering of the first building. Lime and bricks were more plentiful now, so solid brick walls replaced half-timbering in all major building projects. However, log houses would still be built in Salem through the first third of the nineteenth century.

Within two years, fortunately, the Single Sisters moved to a house of their own. A badly needed addition was also built for the Single Brothers' House, doubling its size, and a new Boys' School was constructed. The Brothers made repairs to the water pipes and the mill, and built a stone bridge near the tanyard. Brother Marshall began plans for a new church to hold the growing congregation. The cornerstone was laid on June 12, 1798.

In their new house, the Single Sisters' enterprises flourished. As early as 1788, when outsiders discovered that the Moravians educated girls as well as boys, they began to ask if they could send their daughters to Salem to be educated. Several times over the next few years, as more outsiders urged the Moravians to open their girls' school to boarding students, the Brethren sought the guidance of the Lot. It was not until 1802 that a favorable Lot was drawn and plans could be made to establish a girls' boarding school.

During these years new private dwellings were built as well. The trades flourished as more furniture, ceramics, tools, and utensils were needed by the growing population.

ATTITUDES TOWARD SLAVERY

The Moravians' attitude toward slavery gradually changed after the Revolution. By 1800, individually and collectively, Moravians owned about seventy enslaved Africans and African Americans. Most lived and worked on farms in Bethania, Hope, and Friedberg. Since many chose not to join the Moravian Church, they did not have the 0same advantages as other Africans and African Americans who had been baptized as members of the church.

During the 1790s, mounting discontent among enslaved people throughout the South and in the Caribbean was matched by a growing racial prejudice among whites in the South and elsewhere. Signs of intolerance in the Moravian congregations were at first rebuked by the church elders, who maintained that while matters of class and station had to be honored, "not the slightest distinction between whites and blacks can be made in matters of the spirit."

But the position of the church was changing. The Moravians were influenced by prevailing racist attitudes and by the fear that followed an aborted slave rebellion in eastern North Carolina in 1802 and the successful rebellion of Africans in Haiti during the same time. The church gradually began to practice segregated worship.

TESTING THE RULES

In the aftermath of the Revolutionary War, some Moravians began to test the rules and regulations in their carefully controlled community life. The board overseeing the country congregations warned that too many people were "beginning to feel the spirit of the freedom in the land." The board was concerned that people would lose control of their children and forget their daily devotions. Many began to neglect attendance at the *Singstunden* and other services. Some began to change their views about the church, race, dress, and ways of doing business with each other and with the outside world. By 1800, members of the congregation began to challenge the practice of using the Lot to make decisions, especially about marriages. The church was no longer the central focus of community life.

Until the late eighteenth century, most Moravians in Salem held to traditional dress—dark coats and breeches for the men, and, for women, dresses with petticoats and laced jackets, and the *haube*, a tight-fitting linen cap that tied beneath the chin. The ribbon color a girl wore with her haube changed as she grew up—from cherry red for a little girl, to pink for a Single Sister, to blue for a Married Sister. Widows wore white ribbons.

Before the turn of the century, however, the Salem Moravians had begun to keep step with fashion trends around the country. Some of the younger people began to experiment with fancier clothes for daily life and then to wear these new styles to church. In 1787, their concerned elders officially addressed the problem of the "new fashions which are slipping in among us" and the resulting "lust for fashionable apparel." The church records re-

(Above) Moravian families amused themselves by making music together.

(Left) A late-eighteenth-century watercolor showing the Moravian minister and teacher, Jacob Van Vleck, giving a music lesson to a group of girls under the watchful eye of a Married Sister.

veal that frugal Moravians did not want their young people to squander money or try to draw attention to themselves:

In the first place it should be noted that a desire for fashionable dress is at bottom a wish to wear something different, something new, and so become noticable and attract attention. Among such things are the big, shaggy hats; the hats with drooping brims, down which hang cords, or a pretty ribbon or an unusual buckle. Colors also come under the head when they are chosen to strike the eye, or when they are variegated; or when Clothing is adorned with silver or gilt or other shining buttons, and when coat and vest and breeches each has a conspicuous color.

Furthermore, all were admonished to "dress according to their station, and a poor person should not have the clothes which one more well-to-do might properly purchase."

"There is something agreeable in the singing in the Brethren's meetings, because it is very distant from the otherwise customary loud bawling of the hymns, & thereby becomes the more devout & harmonious."
August Spangenberg, 1772

(Above)
A View of Salem in N. Carolina, *by Ludwig von Redeken, 1787. Although the landscape has changed, many of the buildings in this watercolor are still recognizable. Note the tavern, isolated from the rest of the town at the right, and the brewery and tannery buildings, which have not been reconstructed, at the left.*

(Right)
The steeple of Home Moravian Church, built between 1798 and 1800, rises above the town.

MAKING MUSIC IN SALEM

Some facets of life in Salem remained constant. From the very beginning, music was woven into the ritual and liturgy of the Moravian Church, as well as into daily life. The Moravians brought the first trombones to colonial North America and built the first organs. The *Singstunde*, a church service devoted almost entirely to singing, was an important church ritual.

Salem's musicians played for church services and for special celebrations. The Brothers took their trombones and other brass instruments into the farm fields in autumn to play hymns of thanks for a plentiful harvest. On Easter Sunday they played in God's Acre to celebrate the Resurrection. When the top beam of a new building was lifted into place, a musician climbed aloft to play a hymn of celebration. Musicians also tolled the deaths, or "home-going," of congregation members.

An orchestra organized in Salem in the early 1780s played Mozart and Haydn as well as traditional hymns. A number of Moravians composed secular and religious music. John Frederick Peter, the director of music in Salem from 1780 to 1790, has been called the first composer of chamber music in America.

The Moravians can claim another musical first. The German-born Johann Klemm and David Tannenberg of Lititz, Pennsylvania, were the first organ builders in the American colonies. In 1763 they built an organ for Bethabara, and Tannenberg went on to build two more organs for Wachovia. By 1800 there were three organs in Salem: one in the Gemein Haus, one in the Single Brothers' House, and the magnificent two-manual organ Tannenberg built for Home Church.

Music was an important part of Christmas celebrations in early Salem. For the Moravians, Christmas was a religious celebration that focused on Jesus's birth rather than gift-giving. A lovefeast for children was held on Christmas Eve, with

Johann Gottlob Krause

Johann Gottlob Krause was an orphan, a misfit, and a rebel. Born in Bethabara in 1760, he lost his parents by the time he was two years old and grew up in the care of the Bethabara congregation.

In 1771, master potter Gottfried Aust adopted eleven-year-old Gottlob and took him to Salem as his potter's apprentice. The Salem church council tried to teach the boy to behave properly and obey his elders, for he was stubborn and defiant. Brother Aust could be a tough task master, and Gottlob tried to run away in 1773. Their turbulent relationship continued until 1781, when Gottlob was allowed to learn masonry from Melchior Rasp.

Despite his difficulties with Brother Aust, Gottlob Krause became a master potter as well as a master mason. He ingeniously transferred the techniques and aesthetic taste he learned in the pottery shop to his work as a mason and builder. The brick structures he built were beautiful and well constructed. His trademark was the ornamental use of brickwork: he would accent windows and doors with painted or dark brick, or lay bricks of different colors in distinctive herringbone and chevron patterns.

Brother Krause was responsible for making and laying the bricks for the Single Sisters' House and the Salem Tavern. His handiwork can also be seen in the Boys' School, the Christoph Vogler House, Home Moravian Church, Winkler Bakery, and the Vierling House. Krause emblazoned his own initials in brick on the side of the Christoph Vogler House, in effect leaving his signature for the future.

Gottlob Krause was stubbornly independent, accused at times, rightly or wrongly, of being a horse trader, a thief, and an inconsistent Christian. Most of all, he was a craftsman and builder ahead of his time. Fortunately, his legacy endures in many of the beautiful buildings of Salem.

special readings and music. Back in 1747, in Germany, Bishop Johannes von Watteville had used a beeswax candle wrapped in red paper as a symbol of the "flame of love" kindled by Christ's birth and suffering. At their lovefeast, Salem children would be given similar candles, which they would light at the end of the service.

(Above left) Johann Gottlob Krause set his initials in the brickwork of the Christoph Vogler House.

(Above right) Decorated ceramics, pewter plates, and utensils of wood and metal, many made in Salem, stock an eighteenth-century kitchen cupboard.

(Left) On the porch of the Salem Tavern, two women in eighteenth-century clothing take a break from their work.

55

Salem Tavern

The 1784 Tavern.

"Salem is a small but neat village; and like all the rest of the Moravian settlements, is governed by excellent police,— having within itself all kinds of artizans; —the number of souls does not exceed 200."

George Washington's Diary, 1791

The original tavern, built in 1771, was one of the first public buildings constructed in Salem. The site chosen for it was on the southern outskirts of the settlement because the town elders sought to protect the members of the congregation from the worldly influence of outsiders. Nevertheless, the success of the tavern was important to the town's business interests; a steady flow of travelers depended on it for lodging and food, and Salem merchants and craftsmen relied on their business. The Salem Tavern was soon known throughout the Southeast for its fine hospitality and service.

WELCOME, STRANGER

The Moravians in Salem used the term *Strangers* to refer to people who were not members of the Moravian Church. They were outsiders, to be welcomed but sometimes to be feared. They brought essential business to the tradesmen and the Community Store, but they also brought worldly attitudes and behavior. Over the years, countless Strangers passed through Salem and lodged at the Salem Tavern, where the tavern keeper was instructed to keep them in their "proper places."

According to the "Instructions for the Hosts of Salem Tavern," Salem residents were permitted to take Strangers into the Tavern for food and drink, especially if the Strangers had come to Salem to do business. Congregation members were not permitted, however, to frequent the tavern to "come together for gossip, or loafing, or unnecessary acquaintance with Strangers."

The Salem physicians treated many Strangers, and if a Stranger died during a sojourn in Salem, he or she might be buried in the special graveyard for Strangers, located where St. Philips Church now stands.

During the Revolution, the tavern was kept busy housing and feeding soldiers, British and American alike, and other Strangers. Shortly after the war's end, on the night of January 31, 1784, the tavern was destroyed by fire. By now the tavern was a mainstay of the Salem economy, and rebuilding it took priority over other projects. Using materials that had been gathered to build the Single Sisters' choir house, the Moravians immediately rebuilt on the foundations that had survived the fire. Within the year, the new tavern was ready for business. Once again guests were served "in every respect, in such a way that their consciences must tell them that we are honest and Christian people, such as they have never before found in a tavern."

The Salem Tavern had a reputation far and wide for its hospitality, cleanliness and order, fair prices, and good meals. Merchants and traders who came to Salem to do business spent the night at the tavern, and took their meals there. Parents of students at the Girls' School also stayed there. Families from eastern North Carolina sometimes stopped in Salem on their way to new pioneer settlements in western North Carolina, Virginia, and Tennessee.

A continuous procession of sometimes lively Strangers kept the tavern keeper and his helpers busy. From time to time, when tavern guests got drunk and disorderly, tavernkeeper Jacob Blum's other job as a justice of the peace came in handy. And despite edicts to the contrary, some Salem men visited the tavern to enjoy a glass of brandy or beer and to hear the news of the surrounding settlements and colonies.

Tavern guests were served in the two front rooms that flank the wide central hallway. To the left, travelers of the "lesser sort" would congregate in the Guest Room. They sat at long tables to share the *ordinary*, a standard, inexpensive meal that was served at a designated time each day. Across the hall in the Gentlemen's Room, a more private, comfortable dining room, guests sat at smaller private tables and were served more elaborate meals at their convenience. Overnight guests could rent an upstairs room or a bed in a shared room. The room on the northeast corner, the best bedroom, was probably where George Washington slept when he visited Salem in 1791. The tavern keeper and his family used the back rooms on the first floor for their living quarters.

THE HOSTS OF SALEM TAVERN

From 1772 to 1780, Jacob and Dorothea Meyer ran the tavern for the congregation. The tavern keeper and his wife both had to be hard workers, and they needed the help of a number of other people as well. Of all the businesses in Salem, the tavern was most dependent on the labor provided by African Americans. The Meyers had the help of two enslaved African Americans, an elderly woman called Susy and her daughter, called Cathy, and other workers.

When the Meyers had to give up their work because of poor health, Jacob Blum and his second wife, Maria Elizabeth, came from Bethabara to take over as tavernkeepers in May 1787; they ran the tavern until February 1803. They brought with them their three children, A. Christina, Jacob, and Christian, as well as an enslaved African American couple, Peter and Louisa, and their son Wilhelm.

The work of the tavern was supported by a number of outbuildings, including a barn similar to the one that stands now, and a woodshed. In addition, the tavern was assigned a tract of land equal in size to 27 town lots, where crops were planted and livestock pastured.

Tavern workers grew much of the food that was served to guests, and what was not grown on tavern land was generally produced in Salem or on outlying farms. Beer and brandy from the brewery were stashed in the cool vaulted cellars that had survived from the 1771 tavern

building, as were sides of pork and beef and cured meats and sausages. Wheat and other grains ground at the Salem Mill were stored in the dry attic. Keeping a supply of food and drink on hand was a constant challenge.

DISTINGUISHED GUESTS

The men and women who worked at the church-owned tavern often served guests of distinction. Alexander Martin, the governor of North Carolina, stayed there from time to time. The former governor of Georgia passed through Salem in September of 1791, as did parties from South Carolina and Virginia. After South Caro-

(Above)
The barn, seen from the Tavern Meadow, was moved from the Moravian town of Bethania to Salem in 1961 to the location of the original barn. It dates from the 1820s.

(Center)
The Tavern kitchen, with its open hearth and bake oven.

(Below)
In the Gentlemen's Room, travelers took their meals and socialized in comfortable surroundings.

57

Salem Tavern in 1791

"[The President] talked on various matters with several Brethren . . . in the room that had been prepared for him."

*Salem Diary
June 1, 1791*

On the first morning of his visit to Salem, George Washington is meeting with Frederic William Marshall as the tavernkeeper offers them breakfast. They have just learned that Governor Martin is traveling from Salisbury to meet with the President, so Washington has decided to stay another night. Two of his attendants are planning the next leg of their trip, to Guilford Courthouse, to visit the site of the decisive Revolutionary battle there.

In the kitchen, Sister Blum has just learned of the President's change in plans and is discussing with Louisa, the cook, how they will feed him that evening. What can they use to make a special meal for such a distinguished guest? They had only planned to feed him and his entourage for one day! Peter, Louisa's husband, has come in from overseeing the horses. When Sister Blum and Louisa decide what they will prepare, he will bring supplies up from the vaulted cellar or down from the attic.

At the front of the tavern, people from Salem and other towns gather in hopes of seeing the President. Because the first-floor facade was built without windows, they cannot peer in to see him at his breakfast, but some children try to catch a glimpse of him through the door.

Despite the hubbub of the President's visit, everyday morning tasks have to be done. In the tavernkeeper's private quarters, a servant spins linen thread and sees that Christian Blum completes his schoolwork. The black leather firebuckets in the tavernkeeper's office behind them are reminders of the threat of fire, which destroyed the first tavern in 1784. In the kitchen, a young man pulls baked loaves out of the oven.

Upstairs, Washington's manservant is packing the President's clothing, and another tavern guest is just getting out of bed!

Soon, the President will tour the choir houses and workshops of Salem. The Moravians are eager to show him their well-run town.

"It would be well to have some English books in our tavern, for example the History of the Brethren . . . so that travelers can get a better idea of our church."
Salem Board Minutes January 21, 1791

Salem Tavern

(Above)
The tavernkeeper's bedroom where George Washington may have stayed when he visited Salem, offered all the comforts most travelers would expect in a fine tavern.

(Right)
A ceramic stove, made in Salem, kept the guests' sleeping rooms warm in winter.

by four white coach horses and accompanied by a milk-white saddle horse. Washington was accompanied by his secretary, several outriders, and servants clad in white livery trimmed in yellow. He was greeted by a brass band and a cheering crowd, and Moravian musicians played for him during his evening meal.

Washington had only planned to spend one night in Salem, but when he learned that Governor Alexander Martin was traveling from Salisbury to meet him, he extended his stay. The second day, he visited the Single Brothers' House, the Single Sisters' House, some workshops, and the Boys' School. In the evening, he and Governor Martin attended a *Singstunde* (song service), where the Moravians sang English hymns sent from Pennsylvania especially for the President's visit. The next day, Washington traveled to Guilford Battleground, accompanied to the Wachovia border by Frederic Marshall and the pastor, Ludwig Benzien.

On a festive occasion such as the President's visit, everyone at the tavern had extra work to do. Peter and other stable hands would have cared for the horses. In the hot kitchen, Sister Blum and Peter's wife Louisa would have cooked substantial meals. The President and his party would have been offered the best of the tavern's cellar stock of whiskey, brandy, wine, beer, or cider.

The Moravians made a positive impression on the President. Washington wrote, "I am greatly indebted to your respectful and affectionate expressions of personal regard, and I am not less obliged by the patriotic sentiments contained in your address. From a Society, whose governing principles are industry and the love of order, much may be expected towards the improvement and prosperity of the country in which their Settlements are formed,—and experience authorizes the belief that much will be obtained."

Today you can visit the rooms where guests ate and slept, including the room where President Washington probably stayed. You can watch demonstrations of open-hearth cooking and other household chores that kept the tavern running smoothly.

lina congressman William Loughton Smith's visit and stay at the tavern in the spring of 1791, he described the beauty of Salem's houses and meadows in his diary: "The antique appearance of the houses built in the German style and the trees among which they are placed have a singular and pleasing effect; the whole resembles a beautiful village and forms a pastoral scene."

The tavern's most important guest was President George Washington, who stayed from May 31 to June 2, 1791. He arrived on the afternoon of the 31st in a cream-colored coach with gilt trim, pulled

Architecture Key

Salem Tavern

800 South Main Street. Built 1784; restored 1956. Lot 68.

T · R R · V

Woodshed   Woodshed

The tavern is the first all-brick building in Salem, erected over the vaulted cellar rooms of the 1771 tavern, which was destroyed by fire. The bricks had been ordered for the Single Sisters' House, but were used for the tavern since rebuilding it was considered a priority.

The two-story brick building has interior end chimneys and brick elliptical arches over the windows, and a wooden roof with a kick eave held in place with locking plates. One of the most interesting features is the windowless front wall facing the front porch, presumably designed to prevent townspeople from observing the Strangers within.

The tavern expanded over the years. A two-story wooden-frame wing was added on the southwest side in 1815–16; a second building, which now houses the Salem Tavern restaurant, was built north of the brick tavern in 1816. In 1832, the two buildings were joined by the "dining hall," and in 1838 a two-story porch was built across the facade of all three structures. The dining hall was removed in 1897.

After the brick tavern was donated to the Wachovia Historical Society in 1941, it was partially restored to its 1784 appearance with the help of more than fifty yearly inventories, some dating from before the Revolutionary War.

(Above)
An 1882 photograph of the brick tavern and the wooden 1816 building joined by a two-story connector, called the "dining hall," with a two-story porch running across the facade of all three structures.

(Center)
The 1816 Tavern building (foreground) now houses a restaurant.

(Below)
The Tavern's solid brick facade facing the porch may have been designed to prevent Moravians from looking in on strangers staying at the Tavern.

The Single Sisters' Choir

The Single Sisters' House, seen from Salem Square.

The first Single Sisters who came from Bethabara to Salem in 1772 lived in the Gemein Haus, which also housed the pastor and his family; the Saal, or room for worship; and the school for little girls. The Sisters waited patiently for the end of the Revolution to build a choir house of their own, only to see the materials collected for their house used to rebuild the tavern after it burned to the ground in 1784. Their house was built on the square in 1786. Now part of Salem Academy and College, the Single Sisters' House is not open to the public, but it is a vital part of Salem's history.

The Moravians' choir system gave women a voice in congregation affairs. In the Married Sisters' and Single Sisters' choirs, women could hold positions of authority and have a say in issues that concerned them. Many women wanted marriage and homes of their own, but for those who did not, the Single Sisters' House offered a positive, comfortable setting in which they could be independent and productive.

THE SINGLE SISTERS' CHOIR

The Single Sisters worked together to provide for their own needs, from cooking and housekeeping, to weaving and making clothes, to growing their own food. Each woman or older girl was required to pay for her room, board, clothing, and other personal needs. In addition, the Single Sisters earned money by providing services to the community: operating a laundry, weaving linen, sewing leather gloves, nursing the sick, teaching girls, and, from 1805, running a girls' boarding school.

The Single Sisters' hard work, much of it manual labor, helped to anchor Salem's economy. The church council appreciated and depended on the steady stream of income that poured into the church treasury thanks to the Single Sisters' frugality and perseverance. After the sisters had paid the last installment on the mortgage for their choir house in 1820, their profits helped to support mission projects, the financially struggling Boys' School, and other Moravian enterprises. The church used their profits to settle other congregation debts, including those left after the Single Brothers' House was closed in 1823.

The church council was shocked by the Single Sisters' yearly accounting for 1844, which showed a net profit of 500 dollars, compared to 2,000 dollars a few years earlier. The strong-willed Sisters chose to spend 900 dollars of their funds to pay other workers to do the heavy kitchen labor that year—a decision that the disapproving church fathers challenged as "quite striking."

WOMEN'S WORK IN SALEM

All women in Salem, not only Single Sisters, worked hard. A Married Sister was an equal partner in her husband's work. Maria Elizabeth Blum ran the Salem Tavern alongside her husband, Jacob. Henrietta Miksch's gingerbread was a mainstay of the shop she ran with Matthew. Anna Dorothea Benzien, wife of the pastor Christian Ludwig, helped her husband minister to the congregation's needs. Women also held important positions in the church and on the community's boards.

A Married Sister also ran her household, a full-time job in itself. She had daily chores such as cooking and cleaning, caring for children, and sewing and mending. Some chores, such as baking, laundry, and ironing, were done weekly. Other activities were seasonal. Winter was the time to preserve meats in quantity, and to make dipped candles from tallow and

Sister Maria Steiner Denke

Maria Steiner (1792–1868) has been called the most distinguished educator of young women in Salem in the nineteenth century. Her family background almost dictated that she would be a teacher. Her father, Abraham Steiner, was Inspector of the Girls' Boarding School; her mother, Catherine Sehner, was the second teacher at the Girls' School from 1780 to 1791. Maria, who was called Polly, was one of the first two Salem girls to study at the Girls' Boarding School in Salem when it opened in 1802. She began to teach at the school in 1811, when she was 18.

Polly was always patient and tactful with her students, but she was an independent woman, known for speaking her mind. In 1820, she gave up teaching to take on the larger responsibility of *Pflegerin*, or leader of the Single Sisters. In 1823, however, after she refused to cancel plans for a "recreational trip" with two other Single Sisters and two Single Brothers, Sister Steiner resigned from her position as Pflegerin. The church elders certainly valued her talents, for she was allowed to return to teaching.

Despite the church elders' disapproval, Polly often did things her own way. She gave private music lessons without permission, and once attended a meeting in nearby Waughtown, spending the night. It was no doubt a relief to the church councils when she married the Reverend Christian Friedrich Denke in 1828. She was 36, and he was a 53-year-old widower. They lived for five years in Friedberg, where he was pastor of the Moravian Church, and then returned to Salem.

After her husband's death in 1838, Sister Denke taught music and religion to the African American children of the area. In 1845, she spent two years in France as the governess of two of her former pupils who were studying in a Moravian school there. When she returned to Salem, she added French to the list of subjects that she taught with great success.

Sister Denke was appointed "directress" of the Academy in 1848, a post she held until a few months before her death on November 27, 1868. For years afterward her students praised their unforgettable teacher. As one wrote in 1890, "Many of us owe our aspirations and their higher forms and nobler aims to her wise admonitions and intellectual attainments."

Women's chores ranged from harvesting flax (above) to doing laundry out-of-doors (left).

beeswax. In spring, lye made from ashes was boiled with fat to make soap. Work in the family garden now also began in earnest and continued through the summer, and fruits and vegetables were preserved as they came in season. In summer, in addition to garden work, women helped with haying and harvesting grains and flax. In the fall harvesting and preserving continued, and fruits, especially apples, were dried for winter use.

Clothing a family took much planning and effort. Most women sewed for themselves and their children, and made undergarments for the men and boys in the family. Girls were taught to sew at a young age; by the time they were teenagers, they could make their own clothes.

To prevent the Moravians from seeing themselves as above manual labor and dependent upon the labor of others, the church discouraged families from having

The Single Sisters' Choir

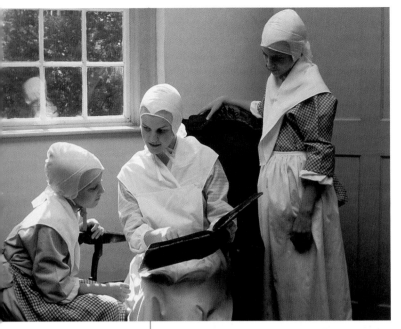

(Above)
Some Single Sisters taught at the Girls' School until they married; others made teaching a lifelong career.

(Right)
Needlework was an important part of the girls' training. This sampler was made by Christina Spach in 1804.

Sister Oesterlein successfully taught and nurtured her charges, and the fledgling school flourished.

Schools for girls were rare in the South, and as early as 1788 outsiders began to ask if they could send their daughters to be educated in Salem. By 1803, plans were well underway to build a boarding school for girls, and the school building was finished in the summer of 1805. Even before the building was completed, however, parents brought their daughters to Salem in hopes of enrolling them in the Boarding School. By the fall of 1805, the student body numbered thirty girls from North Carolina, South Carolina, Georgia, Tennessee, and Virginia. By 1825, enrollment in the school had grown to 114 girls.

In the 1820s, a few Cherokee girls were enrolled in the boarding school. They were the daughters of leaders of the Cherokee Nation and had attended the Moravian school in Springplace, Georgia.

The school building held classrooms, a dining room, a sick room, an attic dormitory for the girls, and living space for the Single Sisters who taught and watched over them. It could accommodate approximately sixty girls. The headmaster, called the Inspector, lived with his family in the boarding school until he was provided his own residence on the square, just across from the church.

The girls took classes in reading, writing, syntax, history, geography, music, drawing, and needlework. From time to time, German was part of the curriculum as well. They took their meals in a large dining hall on the ground floor and slept in the attic dormitory. When they were ill, a Single Sister tended the girls in the special sick room.

During the Civil War many southern families, Moravian and non-Moravian alike, entrusted their daughters to the care of the Salem Female Academy and the Moravian community in Salem, believing they would be safer there than in their own homes. Soon after the Civil War, the school was approved to offer college work as well as the traditional preparatory school program. Today, on a beautiful fifty-six-acre campus, Salem Academy and College sustain the long tradition rooted in Sister Oesterlein's first school.

domestic servants or slaves except in unusual cases. Children were expected to help in the house and the garden. A Single Sister could come and help the woman of the house on an occasional basis as a way of earning her own way. Women often helped each other with seasonal tasks, and in times of sickness or childbirth, women of the community, both Married and Single Sisters, took turns nursing in the sickroom, helping with the household, and tending children.

THE GIRLS' BOARDING SCHOOL

John Amos Comenius (1592–1670), the Moravian bishop and educator, recognized that women were as gifted and capable as men. He insisted that girls be given the same education as boys. In accordance with his ideals, the Moravians were committed to the education of all their children, daughters as well as sons. When Single Sister Elisabeth Oesterlein moved to Salem from nearby Bethabara in 1772, she started a small day school for girls.

Architecture Key

Single Sisters' House 627 Church Street. Built 1786; restored 1974. Lot 15.
Girls' Boarding School 619 Church Street. Built 1805; restored 1966. Lot 14.

The Single Sisters' House shares several features with the 1784 Tavern and the Single Brothers' House addition constructed later in 1786: walls laid in Flemish bond, with dark or burned headers; elliptical relieving arches over the windows; and a "kick" eave on the roof. Rubbed bricks accentuated the decorative brickwork around the windows and doors.

Dormers were added in 1812, and an addition to the southern end in 1819 created space for a Saal and sick rooms. The main section of the building's exterior has been restored to its 1786 appearance and the addition to 1819.

The 1805 Girls' School was the last large brick structure to be built by the con-gregation. Its hooded stoop entrance is original, as is the decorative Flemish bond pattern with glazed headers. Instead of rubbed brick to set off door and window openings, painted brick was used.

In the 1960s, the Girls' School was restored to its 1805 appearance. Alterations made over time were stripped away, including wings that connected it with Main Hall and the Single Sisters' House, and a Victorian facade that matched the roofline of Main Hall. Two nineteenth-century additions were left intact: the northern section of the building, added in 1824, and the clerestory built in 1837.

(Above)
The Girls' Boarding School in an 1840s lithograph, showing the 1837 clerestory (series of windows added at the attic level).

(Left)
The Single Sisters' House in an 1882 photograph.

The arched light with lancet tracery above entry doors was first used on the Single Sisters' House. It is a feature that, with variations, would become common in Salem.

The Single Sisters' House and the Girls' School are part of Salem Academy and College. They are not open to the public.

The Boys' School

(Above)
A classroom as it would have appeared in the early nineteenth century, with long desks and benches, slates, an abacus, and a globe.

(Right)
An illustration from Comenius's Orbis Pictus (View of the World), considered the first picture book for children.

"And so I began today with my service for the school. In Writing and in Arithmetic some of my scholars are already quite advanced, but not so in Reading and English. Gave a piano lesson . . . ."

The Diary of Peter Wolle, head teacher of the Boys' School from 1814 to 1817

Felis clamat, nau nau The *Cat* crieth.		N n
Auriga clamat, ò ò ò The *Carter* crieth.		O o
Pullus pipit, pi pi The *Chicken* peepeth.		P p
Cúculus cuculat, kuk ku The *cuckow* singeth.		Q q
Canis ringitur, err The *dog* grinneth.		R r
Serpens sibilat, si The *Serpent* hisseth.		S s

Salem boys between the ages of about 6 and 14 began attending school in this building after its completion in 1794. They were taught in the Germanic tradition of rigorous academic work and strict discipline. Classes stretched far beyond the three Rs to include Latin, English, and German grammar; geometry and other forms of advanced mathematics; geography; history; religion; music; and penmanship. In addition, the boys were expected to learn such practical skills as sewing on buttons and darning stockings.

Except for Sundays, the boys were encouraged to partake of physical exercise, from swimming and walking to flying kites and playing ball. Strict rules governed even their playtime, however; there was to be no undue noise, no running in the streets, no disregard for the well-being of neighbors.

Most Salem boys slept in the sleeping hall on the third floor but were allowed to go home for certain meals with their parents. Classes were held year round, and lasted for most of the day. At 5:15 on summer mornings and a more leisurely 6:30 on dark winter mornings, students were awakened for breakfast. Promptly at eight o'clock, beds were made and other chores done. Then classes and study hours began in earnest.

Whether they knew it or not, Salem children were being brought up in a church with a history of commitment to education. Jan Amos Comenius, a bishop of the Unity of Brethren, has been called the father of modern education. A champion of enlightened education for children, he advocated such revolutionary ideas as teaching "all things to all men and from all points of view." Many of his visionary principles echoed in Moravian schools throughout the world.

"Every one knows that whatever disposition the branches of an old tree obtain they must necessarily have been so formed from its first growth, for they cannot be otherwise," Comenius wrote in 1631 in his book, *The School of Infancy,* stressing the importance of early childhood education. He also advocated the education of girls as well as boys because, as he wrote, "They are also partakers of the mercy and the kingdom of the future life. . . . In their minds they are equally gifted to acquire wisdom."

The Boys' School now contains exhibits on Moravian history and life in Salem, and there is an early schoolroom on the second floor.

Nearly half the objects on exhibit have been provided by the Wachovia Historical Society, which used the school building as a museum for several decades, beginning in 1897. Here the society stored and displayed its flourishing collection of artifacts, including items gathered by Moravian missionaries in their global travels.

In the early 1950s, Old Salem leased the building, restored it, and took over stewardship of the artifacts in the Wachovia Historical Society's rich collection. This collaboration between the society and Old Salem has enhanced the interiors of many exhibit buildings with authentic furnishings, artifacts, and works of art that the society has preserved over the years.

Architecture Key

The Boys' School

3 East Academy Street. Built 1794; restored 1954. Lot 30.

The Salem Boys' School was built in 1794 by Johannes Gottlob Krause. A master mason and skilled engineer, Krause infused traditional, functional buildings with a more modern look and floor plan. In the design of the Boys' School, for instance, Krause did away with the roof "kick" by placing rafters over the ends of the extended joists, not over the supporting walls. He covered the exposed joists with a coved cornice, an innovation he also used in later Salem buildings.

The most noticeable feature of Krause's craft was his ornamental brickwork. He used dark headers to accent the Flemish bond walls, producing distinctive patterns on the school's west gable.

Features the Boys' School shares with other Salem buildings include the elliptical relieving arches over the doors and windows, and the stuccoed walls of the ground floor, which in this case have incised rather than painted lines to resemble cut stone. Its ceramic tile roof is one of only two original eighteenth-century roofs in Salem.

With the exception of an annex built by the Works Progress Administration in 1937–38, the original structure of the Boys' School was never extensively altered. The annex was removed in 1985, and the school has been restored to its 1794 appearance.

The Boys' School as it looks now, on the corner of Salem Square.

A 1798 view of the Boys' School, with a piazza and gardens behind it, done by Nathaniel Shober, a student at the school.

The windows on the ground floor had solid wood shutters to provide security and privacy.

The diamond pattern on the west gable reflects master mason Krause's artistic eye.

Home Moravian Church

Home Moravian
Church seen from
Salem Square.

The Tannenberg
organ at the
100th anniversary
of Home Moravian
Church in 1900.

*"So many gathered
today that the new,
large, and roomy
Saal could not
begin to hold them;
including the
visitors the number
was estimated as
about two thou-
sand."*

*The Dedication of
the New Church
Building in Salem,
November 9, 1800*

Since 1771, the Moravians had worship-ed in the Gemein Haus, or congregation house, where Main Hall now stands. By 1797, Salem had grown so much that the Saal in the Gemein Haus was no longer large enough to hold the congregation. Frederic William Marshall, the chief administrator for Wachovia, began to draw up plans for a new church building, later to be called Home Church.

Marshall's first choice for a site for the church was, in the tradition of Moravian towns in Europe, a prominent place on the town square. He wanted to place Salem's church on the east side of Salem Square, between the Gemein Haus and the Single Sisters' House. However, another factor influenced the church's final location. More powerful even than the highly respected Brother Marshall was the united voice of the Single Sisters.

Ever since the Single Sisters began their laundry enterprise in 1772, they had dried linens on a bleaching green south of the Gemein Haus. The laundry served the community and was an important economic unit of the Single Sisters' Choir—one of its major business enter-

prises, in fact. It was on this very bleaching green that Brother Marshall proposed to build the church.

The Single Sisters took their opposition to the Elders' Conference, who submitted the question to the Lot. To some this might seem to be an inappropriate clash of the community's spiritual and aesthetic needs with the Single Sisters' mundane yet necessary work. However, this work—and the Single Sisters' good will—were essential for the Moravians, who viewed all worthy tasks as implicitly sacred and, therefore, as God's work.

The Lot rejected both the bleaching green and a building site beside the Boys' School. Finally, it offered an affirmative response to a site to the north of the Gemein Haus, just across from the northeastern corner of the square. Ground was broken in 1798, and the church was dedicated in November 1800.

In keeping with Moravian tradition, the interior of the church was plain, with white plastered walls, hard benches for pews, bare wooden floors, and clear glass windows with white linen curtains. The pews ran the length of the building, facing north. Instead of preaching from a pulpit, the pastor delivered the sermon from a small, slightly raised platform covered by an arched canopy, which was located on the north side of the sanctuary.

The choir system influenced how the Moravians gathered to worship. The men and older boys entered the front door and sat together on the west side of the sanctuary. The women and older girls entered the south door from the Gemein House and gathered on the right side. Children sat together at the front of the church, with a watchful adult seated on each end of the bench. This custom of separating Brothers and Sisters in the sanctuary ended in 1870, and from that time on, families could worship together.

In a gallery above the main entrance stood a magnificent organ, built by master organ builder David Tannenberg of Lititz, Pennsylvania. One of the largest instru-ments that Tannenberg built, this organ was removed from the church in 1910 and replaced. By 2004 it had been restored and installed in the Old Salem Visitor Center. It is one of the most important early American organs in existence.

Architecture Key

Home Moravian Church

529 Church Street. Built 1800; renovated 1870 and 1913. Lot 12.

The church was built of brick with several innovative features: stone window sills, a rounded hood that adorned and protected the main entrance to the church, elliptical arched windows with intricate ogee tracery, and a white cupola with a gilded ball and weathervane atop the steep roof. An ingenious trusswork system held up the roof so that central pillars were not needed for support.

Later renovations transformed the church's interior, but the exterior of the church looks much as it did in 1800. The exceptions are the lowered sills on the side windows and the stained glass windows, changes made in 1870.

In 1870, the interior of the church was completely altered so that the pews faced east rather than north, and the old gallery was replaced by a balcony on the north, west, and south sides. The severe beauty of the early church was supplanted by a more ornate style: handsome stained glass windows were installed, and decorative painting accented the organ and moldings.

When the building was expanded to the north in 1913, another balcony was built around the west, south, and east sides, so that the church more than doubled its seating capacity to eight hundred. The Tannenberg organ was replaced by a Kimball organ at that time.

(Above)
The interior of Home Moravian Church in the 1860s, showing the Tannenberg organ on the gallery, before the extensive renovations of the late nineteenth century. The pews are in their original configuration, facing north.

(Left, top)
The west doorway to the church in a 1920s photograph, with the intricate tracery window, the hood over the door, and the graceful wrought iron handrail.

(Left, bottom)
The original weathervane, with its finial of acanthus leaves, high atop the cupola over the church.

From Easter through Thanksgiving, Home Moravian Church is open to visitors Mondays through Fridays from 1:30 to 3:30. For more information, call 336-722-6171.

6. Salem from 1800 to 1850

Our Wachovia congregations will always remember in a special manner the eighteenth century, in which they were founded and brought to their present position. Through dangers within and without our Lord has brought them, has held them to the purpose of their founding, has brought them back when they strayed away, and has never left them without faithful leaders, men and women.

Memorabilia of the Congregations of the Brethren in Wachovia, 1800

The year 1800 was a pivotal one for Salem. Home Church rose above the square, a fitting culmination of the half-century of work, sacrifice, and struggle that shaped Wachovia. Around this time, two outstanding figures of eighteenth-century Salem died: Traugott Bagge in 1800, and Frederic William Marshall in 1802. A new generation of leaders emerged in church and business affairs: Lewis David de Schweinitz, who was the Administrator of Wachovia from 1812 to 1821; Dr. Samuel Vierling; and silversmith John Vogler.

Inevitably, Moravian life would undergo profound changes in the first half of the nineteenth century. The church was gradually compelled to ease its control over the daily life of the congregation. More and more often, religious and secular interests collided. The Lot was gradually eliminated as a means for approving marriages and other decisions.

In 1823, the Single Brothers closed their choir house and their communal businesses. This step was taken partly because the Brothers were unable to make a profit, and partly because of complaints about the younger Brothers' unruly behavior. The Single Brothers' House was used first as a school and then, until 1960, as a house for widowed women.

The Single Sisters, in the meantime, persevered in their work, taking in the laundry of the community and educating little girls. They saved enough money to begin building the Girls' Boarding School in 1805, and periodically loaned money to the church to help with the Single Brothers' debts.

When the Single Brothers' House closed, young men who had finished their apprenticeships had to find other places in Salem to house their work. Sometimes a Single Brother who wanted to set up a business built a small workshop where he would both live and work. Once he had saved enough money, he would build a separate dwelling house and, generally, marry. The gabled workshops you now see date from the 1820s and 1830s. Not all workshops predated the houses of their owners, however; Samuel Shultz's shoe shop was built after his house, probably to provide more room for the family.

As the nineteenth century progressed, there was an increase in privately owned businesses, and a number of people in Salem would become wealthy. Now some Moravians, such as the John Vogler fam-

Mourning embroidery, a popular motif in the early nineteenth century, probably made by Matilda Winkler, daughter of the baker Christian Winkler, c. 1831.

ily, could afford finer houses and clothes, and spent more time and money on travel and the arts. This level of comfort would not have been possible—or even encouraged—in earlier years.

THE INDUSTRIAL REVOLUTION

Business was booming in Salem during the 1830s. In 1835, Salem residents could trade with three hatters, three gunsmiths, two clockmakers, two shoemakers, a toymaker, several confectioners, and several joiners and tinsmiths. Thriving new factories in Salem, including the Meinung and the Nissen carriage works, used new technology and were planned on the large scale mandated by the Industrial Revolution. There was increasing interest in manufacturing tobacco products.

In 1837, during the cotton boom in the South, the Brethren built a cotton factory on a tract of land west of Salem. They equipped their new factory with the latest machinery to produce thread and cloth, expecting to enhance trade and industry in Salem. Although the Brethren brought in outside investors, they wanted to keep most of the profits for themselves and the congregation. They still believed that as few dollars as possible should go into the hands of Strangers.

The Brothers appointed 24-year-old Francis Fries to be superintendent of the cotton factory. Brother Fries, who married John Vogler's daughter Lisetta, was a far-sighted businessman whose energy and enterprise would transform the way business was done in Salem. By 1840, when the cotton mill was running successfully, he left it to build his own wool carding factory. Under a special agreement with the congregation, Brother Fries hired enslaved African Americans from his father to work in the factory. By 1842 he had expanded his equipment, adding spinning machines and, in 1843, hand looms. His mill produced popular heavy jeans cloth, inexpensive lindseys, and more costly fine dyed woolens.

During the American Revolution, Salem weavers and tailors had hand-produced clothing for colonial soldiers to wear. During the Civil War, however, many Confederate soldiers would march in uniforms made from the sturdy gray

cloth produced by machines whirring in the Fries mills.

BROTHER BLUM'S BANK

Step by careful step, whether through trading with faraway cities, accepting investors in the cotton mill, or employing outsiders in the mills and other areas of business, the Moravians were compelled to join the outside world in the rapidly escalating march of progress. In 1815, the Brethren allowed an outside bank, the Bank of Cape Fear in Wilmington, North Carolina, to open an office in Salem, replacing the congregation store as the town's financial clearinghouse.

John Christian Blum was appointed the local agent for the Bank of Cape Fear in 1816. Brother Blum was also Salem's first printer; he purchased a printing press in 1827, planning to combine the two careers of banker and printer. Unfortunately, a fire abruptly ended his career as town banker. On December 21, 1827, he was

The John Blum House (above, left) home of Salem's first commercial bank and first print shop, now houses a gift shop.

Elias Vogler's work box, with his artist's materials and examples of his miniature portraits, is displayed in his bedroom in the John Vogler House.

71

(Above)
The Salem Cotton Mill, in a detail from a drawing made in 1839, two years after the mill was built.

(Right)
1841 broadside advertising Francis Fries's wool-carding mill.

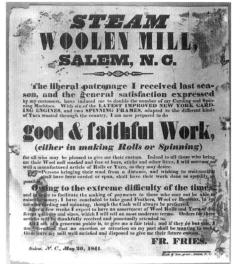

counting out a stack of paper money in the bank room in his home when the time came for the evening service at Home Moravian Church. Brother Blum stopped his work, left the currency on his counting table, and walked to the church, planning to finish his banking tasks later. Within a short time he got the frightening news that his house was on fire. Although his house was saved, ten thousand dollars in currency went up in flames.

This disaster haunted Brother Blum for years. To settle the matter, he had to deed his assets to the Aufseher Collegium, pledging his house, his carriage, and his furniture, including his piano; his printing presses, fonts of type, and paper; and about four thousand pounds of tobacco.

Brother Blum went on to publish the first newspapers in Salem: the *Gleaner*, from 1829 to 1830; the *Farmers' Reporter*, from 1832 to 1837; and the *Carolina Gazette*, from 1840 to 1842. From 1829 he also printed the popular *Farmers' and Planters' Almanac*, which continues to be published to this day as *Blum's Almanac*.

A SCHOLARLY CURIOSITY

A number of Salem residents, including the community botanists, physicians, ministers, and musicians, kept up with the latest developments in the rest of the United States and in Europe. Dr. Samuel Vierling applied the findings of Edward Jenner and other medical researchers to his practice in Salem. Samuel Kramsch, the Inspector of the Boys' School, was an active botanist, as was the Reverend Lewis David de Schweinitz, who served as administrator of Wachovia from 1812 to 1821. A minister and an able administrator, de Schweinitz was also a brilliant botanist. He has been called the father of American mycology (the study of fungi such as mushrooms, mildews, molds, and rusts).

De Schweinitz was one of the most effective ambassadors of the Moravian Church on two continents, thanks to his work as scholar, teacher, artist, minister, and administrator. He was held in such esteem in North Carolina that he was asked to serve as president of the University of North Carolina, an honor he declined because of his devotion to the Moravian Church and his duties in Wachovia. When the North Carolina General Assembly elected him a trustee of the university in 1819, Brother de Schweinitz accepted.

THE ARTS FLOURISH

During the first half of the nineteenth century, an increase in leisure time encouraged more attention to the arts. Artists such as Daniel Welfare (1796–1841) and Elias Vogler (1825–1876) painted portraits and recorded the landscape and vistas of Wachovia. Welfare studied painting in Philadelphia, where he developed a lasting friendship with the prominent artist Thomas Sully. Back in Salem, he painted portraits of Salem residents, including the Charles Bagge family, as well as some religious paintings and landscapes. Elias Vogler, son of the silversmith John Vogler, painted miniature portraits of his family and Salem neighbors, as well as several landscapes.

Women and girls had more time for fancy needlework, from samplers to beaded purses to elaborate mourning embroideries in silk. Many girls, such as Christina Kramsch, daughter of Girls' School Inspector Samuel Kramsch, painted detailed watercolor studies of flowers and other botanical specimens.

Increasing leisure time also encouraged the enjoyment of flowers for their own sake. Pleasure gardens were planted at the Girls' and Boys' schools early in the century. In private households, vivid, well-groomed flower gardens joined the mixed gardens that provided food and medicinal herbs.

During the Christmas season, Salem families such as the Voglers would decorate their houses with greenery and make a Christmas *putz* (from the German verb *putzen*, to decorate) displaying the nativity scene. Since the Christmas tree became popular in German homes in the nineteenth century, some Salem families may have had small trees on tabletops, decked with handmade ornaments. Families and friends would share simple gifts and traditional Christmas cakes, as well as special music for the season. All the people of the town, including the children, would attend the Christmas Eve lovefeast in the church, which was decorated with cedar boughs or other greenery.

The nineteenth-century Moravians did not abandon their church's interests beyond Salem. The local Society for the Propagation of the Gospel Among the

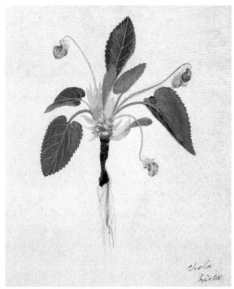

(Above) Daniel Welfare's oil portrait of the Charles Bagge family, painted in 1825. Note how different the clothing is from earlier dress.

(Left) Watercolor of a violet plant by Christina Kramsch, painted around 1810 while she was a student at the Girls' School.

Heathen sent missionaries to begin a school for Cherokee children in Springplace, Georgia, in 1801. The Cherokee and the Moravians gradually learned to trust and respect each other, and many Cherokee leaders visited Salem. Some sent their daughters to the Girls' School. In the 1830s, when the Cherokee were forced to give up their property and move west, the Moravians lobbied the U.S. government in vain to allow their Cherokee friends to stay on their ancestral homelands.

Life in the United States changed considerably in the first half of the nineteenth century, and life in Salem kept pace with the industrial revolution and other social developments. Salem was being transformed with the times, but it still remained above all a Moravian community. Inevitably, however, even this would change.

The Winkler Bakery

Cutting out cookies to be baked in the wood-fired oven.

Patience Cakes

Take 1-1/2 lbs. sugar, 1 dozen eggs, the whites have to be well beaten with a little oil of lemon and 1-1/4 lbs. flour. Work until it is feather light. Bake.

Winkler family recipe

A nineteenth-century cookie cutter.

In the eighteenth century, the Single Brothers operated the town bakery. The town elders frowned on this arrangement, however, because Single Sisters had to purchase their daily bread from Single Brothers unchaperoned. Consequently, in 1799 the Aufseher Collegium chose the Married Brother Thomas Butner to be the new baker. Brother Butner hired Gottlob Krause to build a bakery with a living area for his family.

Unfortunately, Brother Butner seemed to prefer farming and shoemaking to baking, and congregation leaders were not happy to discover that he was selling hard cider to the youths of the town. In November 1807, they brought from Pennsylvania a new baker, the Swiss-born Christian Winkler. He bought the bakery and dwelling house from Brother Butner in 1808.

Brother Winkler had come to Nazareth, Pennsylvania, from Germany in 1799. He had directed the bakery operations for the Single Brothers, first in Nazareth and then in Lititz. As a 41-year-old bachelor, he understood that he would have to be married to run the bakery. Soon after his arrival, the Elders Conference proposed 25-year-old Elizabeth Danz, recently come to Salem from Pennsylvania to teach at the Girls' School, as an appropriate wife. The marriage was accepted by the Lot, and Brother Winkler and Sister Danz were married on December 6, 1807. They had six children: Carl Augustus, William, Christian Henry, Louis, Matilda, and Henrietta.

Brother Winkler was hard-working and experienced at his trade, and his 30-year tenure as Salem's baker was a successful one. He and his family baked bread, buns for the lovefeast celebrations, and other goods.

The Winklers would live and work in this house for the rest of their lives. When Brother Winkler began suffering from asthma, his sons carried on the work of the bakery. In the fall of 1827, the Winklers' second son, William, officially took over his father's business. The eldest son, Carl Augustus, had died just before he turned 18, and the third son, called Henry, was a rebel who had been chastised for his "too liberal use of spirituous liquor." Henry Winkler eventually opened his own confectioner's shop in Salem.

Elizabeth Winkler died in 1836 after a lingering illness, and Christian Winkler died of asthma in 1839 at the age of 72. William Winkler and his descendants resided and worked in the bakery for generations afterward, until 1926.

The domed bake oven at Winkler Bakery is typical of bake ovens used in Salem, both in public buildings such as the Tavern and the Single Brothers' Workshop, and in private homes such as the Vierling House. The bakery's oven is still heated with wood as it was nearly 200 years ago.

Today, visitors to the bakery can see Salem bakers at work. The night before baking, the oven is filled with stacks of wood, which are lighted early in the morning. When the wood burns down and the bricks lining the top of the oven are white-hot (about 600° F), the embers are swept away. While the oven cools to between 350° and 450° F, the bakers knead bread dough, mix sugarcake, and cut out cookies. Timing and experience help them gauge when the oven is ready. They bake bread first while the oven is hottest. When the round loaves—up to ninety-six at one time—come out of the gradually cooling oven, the Moravian sugarcake goes in. The last baking of the day, when the oven heat is dying away, is reserved for sugar cookies cut in fanciful shapes.

Architecture Key
The Winkler Bakery
527 South Main Street. Built 1800; restored 1968. Lot 31.

The bakery shares several architectural characteristics with the Boys' School, built by Gottlob Krause six years before: the stuccoed walls of the first story, with painted lines to resemble mortar joints in cut stone; the ornamental brickwork; the relieving arches over the windows; the chimney construction; and the tile roof. The bakery's ground floor houses the work areas and shop. The floors above it served as living space for the baker and his family.

The 1800 Winkler Bakery still offers baked goods for sale as it did over two hundred years ago.

The wood-fired bake oven is a domed structure on the side of the building, made of brick and covered with stucco. Attached to the main chimney is a "squirrel-tail" flue (so called because it curves over the domed top of the oven the way a squirrel's tail curls over its back).

A porch was added to the back of the house in 1818, and over the years a number of outbuildings and bake ovens were added. In 1968 Old Salem restored the property, rebuilding the bake oven and restoring both the exterior and the interior to their 1818 appearance.

The street floor of the Winkler Bakery is open to the public, and no ticket is needed to enter. Visitors may see the bake oven in use and buy bread and sugarcake still warm from the oven, as well as other baked goods. A restaurant on the second floor offers sandwiches and other light fare.

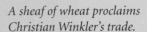

A sheaf of wheat proclaims Christian Winkler's trade.

Sugar cookies and a wreath decorate a window of the bakery at Christmas time.

A squirrel-tail flue on the bake oven at the Salem Tavern.

The Vierling House

(Above)
*The Vierling
House, built by
Johann Gottlob
Krause in 1802.*

(Right)
*The Vierling
Wash-Bake House,
with decorative
brickwork, tile roof,
and a domed oven.*

The Vierling House, one of the finest private dwellings in Salem, was built by Dr. Samuel Benjamin Vierling as a home for his large family and his thriving medical practice.

Dr. Vierling was the most renowned of Salem's early physicians. He was born in Germany in 1765, the child of wealthy Lutheran parents. He joined the Unity of Brethren while studying medicine in Berlin. In the fall of 1789, after completing his studies at the age of 24, Brother Vierling was called to Salem as *medicus*, or physician. Salem had been without a phy-

sician for two years, and the town eagerly welcomed its new young doctor. He arrived in Salem in 1790 and quickly won the confidence of the people of the town and the surrounding areas.

Dr. Vierling was a remarkably skillful surgeon. With little if any anesthesia for his patients, he pulled teeth, amputated gangrenous limbs, removed cataracts, operated for cancer or other maladies, and even performed brain surgery. He also delivered babies, trained midwives, and bled and purged his patients as need be. In addition, he was an herbalist and gardener, growing and then mixing the right proportions and blends of medicinal herbs. These were carefully stored in ceramic jars.

Modern visitors to the doctor's house can admire the well-stocked apothecary shop where Dr. Vierling and his assistants dispensed medicine. In an exhibit of early medical practices upstairs, visitors can shudder at the array of then-modern medical tools, techniques, and instruments Dr. Vierling used to treat his patients.

Dr. Vierling kept informed of the latest international developments in medicine. He began inoculating Salem residents against smallpox after Edward Jenner published his findings about vaccinations in 1798. The good doctor was also a pioneer in dealing with dietary causes of illnesses. When he suspected a connection between the high incidence of stroke in Salem and the high consumption of salt pork, he suggested that the town establish a central meat market so that more fresh meat would be available. The townsfolk took him seriously and built the Market-Fire House in 1803.

In 1790, soon after his arrival in Salem, Dr. Vierling married Anna Elizabeth Bagge, the daughter of Traugott and Rachel Bagge. They settled into married life in the First House in Salem, where physicians before him had kept their homes and the town apothecary shop. Anna Elizabeth died in March 1792, leaving Samuel with their only child, Maria Rosina, a busy practice, and a lonely house.

In August 1792, Dr. Vierling married Single Sister Martha Elizabeth Miksch, the only daughter of Matthew and Henrietta Miksch. Martha cared for little Maria Rosina as if she were her own, and she and Samuel soon had other children. Their first daughter, Henrietta, was born in 1793. The Vierlings would have three sons and five daughters in all. Dr. Vierling was known in Salem as a "tender, loyal, and considerate father for all his house."

The large family quickly outgrew the First House. In 1801, Dr. Vierling asked master builder Johann Gottlob Krause to build a substantial brick house on the hill near God's Acre. Martha and Samuel had chosen the site in February 1801. Their beautiful house would be the last one built by Krause.

They occupied the house on June 5, 1802, filling it with music, children, and medicine. Both Martha and Samuel loved music. Martha had a beautiful voice. Encouraged by her step-grandfather, Bishop Spangenberg, she had memorized "a rich treasury of hymns" from the time she was a child. Samuel loved to play the violin and served the congregation with his musical as well as his medical gifts.

The parlor in the Vierling House now is furnished with a pianoforte, as well as Dr. Vierling's books and some of the music he owned and played. The room also contains furniture that probably belonged to the Vierlings, including a side table and a handsome desk made by Single Brother Johannes Krause.

The large kitchen is furnished as it might have been when the Vierlings lived in the house. Across the wide hallway, the dining room is graced by Windsor chairs—one that belonged to the Vierlings, and five exact reproductions patterned on that surviving chair. You may also see the Vierling family tea kettle, kettle stand, and pearlware coffee pot. The alarm-type clock was made by Salem clockmaker Ludwig Eberhardt. This room sometimes doubled as a bedroom for family members or visitors, especially if someone was ill. Today in this room you may see some of the activities the Vierlings enjoyed, such as painting watercolors, making music, and practicing penmanship.

In the Vierlings' time, many household chores took place outdoors. Behind the Vierling House today, Old Salem interpreters perform some of these activities—straining lye from ashes, making soap over an open fire, washing clothes,

Dr. Vierling's apothecary contained medical implements such as scales, lancets for letting blood, and amputation saws (above) and herbs and other ingredients for medicines that the doctor prepared himself (left).

and baking bread in the domed oven of the Wash-Bake House.

In 1805, the worsening health of Sister Vierling's elderly parents, Matthew and Henrietta Miksch, prompted the Vierlings to move them into their home. With the help of Brother and Sister Opitz, they cared for the Miksches until their deaths several years later.

Perhaps the most profound shock of Sister Vierling's life came in 1817, when her husband died after an epidemic of typhoid fever. That summer brought a particularly virulent epidemic of the disease to Salem, and the 52-year-old physician

The Vierling House

The kitchen in the Vierling House.

Portrait of Friedrich Benjamin Vierling, a son of Samuel and Martha, by Daniel Welfare, 1820–30. Benjamin, as he was called, was a shoemaker. He died in 1827 at the age of 23.

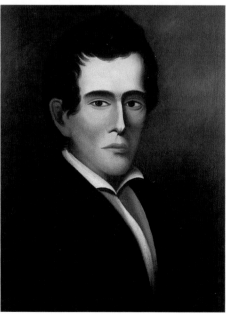

was a victim of the disease himself. As was the Salem way, family and friends surrounded him and sang his favorite hymns as he lay dying. Dr. Vierling's "home-going" happened on November 11, 1817.

In 1819, Sister Vierling left her big house on the hill to move into the Widows' House, and then to live with first one and then another of her children. Around 1828 she lived with her youngest son in the Miksch House where she had grown up.

Sister Vierling ventured to Pennsylvania to visit one of her daughters in 1828 and in 1840, when she was 71. She was "lively and busy" until she suffered a "hard fall in the yard" in 1842. The accident set off severe pains and "dropsy," and her suffering grew so intense that Sister Vierling had to sit up in a chair "long, painful hours of the day and night." She died on February 20, 1844. Not long before her death, Sister Vierling "expressed the wish that as little as possible might be said about her" after she was gone. Fortunately, her children recorded her life in a memoir, celebrating her family history and her contributions as teacher, wife, mother, and grandmother.

After Dr. Vierling's death, a thorough inventory was made of the items in the house. This made it possible to authentically resurrect domestic details as the Vierling House was restored. Descendants of the family also contributed many interesting artifacts that are thought to have belonged to Dr. Vierling, his wife, and their children—the original Windsor chair in the dining room, for example, the portrait of Friedrich Benjamin Vierling, and the tea table in the parlor.

Architecture Key

The Vierling House

463 Church Street. Built 1802. Lot 7.

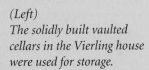

Barn

The Vierling House has a five-bay, center-hall plan with interior chimneys on each end. It is the largest of Johann Gottlob Krause's buildings.

Krause built the walls of the Vierling House in Flemish bond with glazed or darkened headers; the gables were laid in a decorative chevron pattern. As a further accent, Krause used yellow-painted bricks to highlight the quoins (bricks forming the corners of the walls) and the brickwork surrounding all the windows and doors. The front door has an arched hood over a window with ogee tracery.

At the Vierling House you can visit several outbuildings of interest. The original 1831 Wash-Bake House has decorative brickwork, a domed bake oven, and a tile roof to reduce the chance of fire. Here and in the swept yard behind the house, household tasks, including soapmaking, laundry, and baking, are demonstrated.

The 1804 wood-frame barn, which was reconstructed in accordance with archaeological evidence and nineteenth-century photographs, now is used for a video theater and restrooms. You can also see the foundations of the small house occupied by Christian David, an enslaved African American who worked for the church Administrator, Henry Schultz. He lived here from 1835 until his death in 1839. This is the only documented abode of an African American in Salem.

(Above)
A nineteenth-century photograph looking toward the Vierling House and Barn along Church Street.

(Left)
The solidly built vaulted cellars in the Vierling house were used for storage.

Painted brick accenting the windows of the Vierling House.

The Vogler House

(Top)
The John Vogler
House, built
in 1819.

(Above)
Daguerreotype of
John and Christina
Vogler made in
1851.

The wedding ring
John Vogler made
for his bride,
Christina, bears
the words "With
God and Thee My
Joy shall be."

The silversmith and watchmaker John Vogler was, after Traugott Bagge, the most resourceful businessman in Salem. He and his family lived in this house beginning in 1819. The Vogler House illustrates the comfort and cultural advantages many Moravians enjoyed in the mid-nineteenth century.

John Vogler was born in 1783 in Friedland, a Moravian settlement near Salem. He was trained as a gunsmith by his uncle, Christoph Vogler, and learned the craft of silversmithing from him and from craftsmen in Pennsylvania.

In 1809, John Vogler moved into the Single Brothers' House, where he operated a watchmaking and silversmithing shop. Even as a young man he was an astute businessman, importing watches and clocks for resale.

In 1814, John sought permission to marry Single Sister Christina Spach, but the Lot was negative. During the next four years, he made six other marriage proposals regarding five other women. Each of his suggestions was rejected by the Lot

except one, and that Sister, who lived in Pennsylvania, turned him down. John, in the meantime, continued to live and work in the Single Brothers' House.

Finally, in 1818, the Moravians gave up the use of the Lot for deciding marriages between lay church members. Back to the Elders' Conference went John Vogler with a second request to marry Christina Spach, his choice four years earlier. This time his proposal was approved, and Christina accepted immediately. The couple was married on March 7, 1819. John designed a beautiful wedding ring for his bride, three delicate circles of gold with two clasped hands that parted to reveal a double heart inscribed "With God and Thee My Joy shall be."

A NEW HOUSE FOR A NEW ERA

John set to work in 1819 building a house on the lot he had leased from the Moravian Church. This lot was also the site of the smaller frame house that had belonged to Salem's surveyor Gottlieb Reuter and his wife Anna Catharina. Anna Catharina, who had remarried twice after Reuter's death, had spent the end of her days as a widow in that house. It was moved to the back of the lot in 1819, and John and Christina Vogler lived there while their large Federal-style brick house was being built.

John Vogler's house was one of the finest in Salem. Like Vogler himself, it expresses a nineteenth-century independence from many of the styles and ways of eighteenth-century Salem. Influenced by his travels to Philadelphia and other Pennsylvania cities, Vogler chose to build a house in the Federal style—a departure from the Germanic structures that defined Salem at that time.

The house boasts a wide central hall, with four spacious rooms on each floor. About half of the furniture now in the house actually belonged to the Vogler family. Much of it reflects the best Moravian craftsmanship of the time. The tall case and mantel clocks were made by John Vogler's rival, Ludwig Eberhardt, and his son Lewis. The handsome tester bed in an upstairs bedroom is attributed to Moravian cabinetmaker Karsten Petersen. In the parlor are portraits of Christina and John

Vogler painted around 1830 by the Salem artist Daniel Welfare. The wallpaper in the parlor and the bedroom gave a touch of refinement that few Salem houses could boast.

An artist as well as a craftsman, Vogler was responsible for several exterior details that reflect his pride in his craft. He made the brass doorknob, shaped like a fist holding a rod, that graces the front door. He also designed the pedimented hood over the front door, with its decorative glass fan and the painted clock face that advertised his trade.

A SUCCESSFUL BUSINESSMAN

In his silversmithing shop in a front room of his new house, John Vogler's business grew far beyond what he had achieved in the Single Brothers' House. Part of his success lay in his versatility. He worked with different metals, making and selling a wide array of objects. In silver he made graceful, functional spoons and ladles, fancy snuffboxes, and jewelry. He also made gold jewelry.

In brass he crafted such objects as a gold-plated lancet for the doctor to use to draw blood, and a fine surveyor's compass. Although many of these items were functional, Brother Vogler made them beautiful as well. He also did a thriving business selling silverware and other specialty items that he ordered from Philadelphia and other major cities.

Despite the fact that Ludwig Eberhardt was the town's chief clockmaker, Brother Vogler repaired watches and clocks. The Board of Supervisors allowed Vogler to compete with Brother Eberhardt because he worked faster and produced work that was almost as fine as Eberhardt's, and he often charged less money.

The inventiveness and artistic turn of mind that made John Vogler a successful businessman are visible in his private pursuits, as well. He made a physiognotrace, an instrument for tracing profiles or silhouettes. It consisted of a long wand attached to a box that had a sheet of paper on the inside face. When the artist outlined a sitter's profile with one end of the wand, the other end would trace the contours on the paper inside the box. Physiognotraces were used by profile artists in

Silhouettes of Christina and John Vogler

many cities, but having one in Salem would have been a novelty. John Vogler became skillful at this craft, rendering many silhouettes of his family and friends.

Although John was a very modern businessman, he was devoted to the traditions of the Moravian Church. He and Christina were both active in church affairs. Among other activities, for thirty years they were involved with establishing Sunday schools in towns in Wachovia. In 1829, John spent two months away from his business to work as a missionary at the Moravian Cherokee missions at Springplace and Oochgelogy, Georgia.

(Top) Portrait of Lisetta Vogler and her husband, Francis Fries, by Gustavus Grunewald, 1839.

(Above, left) Tracing a profile, or silhouette, with Vogler's physiognotrace.

*(Above)
In John Vogler's shop, reproductions of his original workbench and tools are used to make silver spoons.*

*(Right)
The wallpaper in the parlor and the pianoforte, among other things, set the Vogler's lifestyle apart from that of earlier generations in Salem.*

THE VOGLER FAMILY

John and Christina Vogler had three children: Lisetta, born in 1820; Louisa, born in 1822; and Elias, born in 1825. These children lived lives in the nineteenth century that were very different from those of children in the early days of Salem. The quality of the education they received was better because Salem teachers were now better trained. They enjoyed luxuries that their father's successful business could provide, including opportunities to travel. On one two-month-long trip in 1831, the Voglers visited Washington, Bethlehem, Lititz, Philadelphia, and New York.

In her diary, the 11-year-old Lisetta recorded many details of their journey, including the towns they passed through, the friends they visited, and the varying quality of their meals and accommodations. In New York she was impressed by the city hall, "the Museum 4 stories high with a great Cosmaramo [an observatory], in the upper story and from the top of which we had a most elegant view of the city, waters, shipping, &c.," and "this now beautiful illuminated Broadway so splendid that father said it was far superior to any street in Philadelphia."

Lisetta, Louisa, and Elias were all artistically inclined. Elias's artist's workbox can be seen in his upstairs bedroom; he was a talented miniature painter on ivory. In addition to developing skills as an artist, architect, and sign painter, he took over his father's business in 1848. Lisetta and Louisa did dainty needlework pictures and watercolors. Artworks created by the children can still be seen in the house.

Lisetta married Francis Fries, who established the first textile factory in Salem and played an important role in transforming Salem into a major industrial center. Elias, who married Emma Reich, also contributed to this development. He had successful careers as a silversmith, businessman and architect, and as the second mayor of Salem. In the 1860s he served as superintendent of the Sunday school at St. Philips Church.

Louisa followed the way of the church, marrying the Reverend Edwin Senseman, who was called to be deacon at the Moravian community of Friedberg, south of Salem. In 1852 they moved to the Moravian town of New Salem, Illinois. Louisa, who had been sickly for much of her adult life, died there in 1854 at the age of 32.

Christina Spach Vogler died in this house in 1863, at the age of 70. Her husband John died at the age of 97, in 1881. In the course of two generations, he and his descendants helped Salem grow from a town of artisans to a modern business and industrial center.

Architecture Key
The Vogler House
700 South Main Street. Built 1819; restored 1954. Lot 64.

When John Vogler acquired the rights to Lot 64, it was occupied by a small house built in 1771 by surveyor Christian Gottlieb Reuter for himself and his wife, Anna Catherina. John Vogler had the house moved to the back of the lot, and he and his wife lived there while their new house was being built.

The Vogler House is built of brick, employing the traditional Flemish bond, but with curious flaws in its application. For example, the masons either omitted "closure" bricks at the corners of the walls, or laid the bricks so that every other course needed a brick fragment to finish off the row.

Many features represent the latest styles in 1819. Instead of the arched elliptical window heads seen in many Salem houses, the John Vogler House has straight-head lintels composed of wedge-shaped bricks. Instead of a traditional coved cornice, it has an ornamental cornice with "saw-tooth" brick-work. It has slim, symmetrical gable chimneys. Rather than an arched window over the "Dutch" door, there is a rectangular window with X-patterned panes.

The John Vogler House remained in the family until the early 1950s, when it was donated to Old Salem and restored to its 1819 appearance.

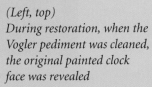

(Above)
The pediment over the front door of the John Vogler House, with a painted clock face indicating his trade.

(Left, top)
During restoration, when the Vogler pediment was cleaned, the original painted clock face was revealed

(Left, bottom)
Door handle made by John Vogler in the shape of a fist and rod.

The Anna Catherina House, now on the back of the Vogler lot, originally stood on Main Street.

The Shultz Shoemaker Shop

Today, shoemakers in Old Salem make shoes just as they were made in the early nineteenth century.

"Today I made a pair of square toed shoes for myself, square toed shoes are now getting in fashion here in the North they have been worn for some years."

John Henry Leinbach's Journal, June 19, 1830

Salem shoemaker Samuel Shultz was born in 1781 in Salem. He served an apprenticeship as a shoemaker and practiced his craft in the Single Brothers' House. In 1819 he married Christina Hein; in the same year he built a frame house (now a private residence) that contained their living space as well as his workshop. For eight years, Shultz ran his shop in the house itself.

In 1827, however, with the permission of the Board of Supervisors, Brother Shultz built a small frame workshop adjoining his house to the north, replicating the exterior details of his house.

Shultz was an enterprising businessman, importing shoes to sell as well as making shoes to order for men, women, and children in Salem. He continually cast about for other, more exotic business enterprises, sometimes with troublesome results. His efforts at raising silkworms proved disappointing in the 1840s. Later, town officers foiled his efforts to sell hard liquor, especially since Brother Shultz had failed to apply for permission ahead of time.

Shultz was not the only shoemaker in Salem. A master craftsman made shoes in the Single Brothers' House until it was closed in 1823. Married Brother John Henry Leinbach, who lived on Main Street north of the square, also worked as a shoemaker at the same time as Shultz. Leinbach kept an extensive diary filled with details about his business, which help us understand the life of an artisan-businessman in early nineteenthcentury Salem.

In Samuel Shultz's shoemaker's shop, costumed interpreters demonstrate his trade, working by hand with the lasts, hammers, and awls that an early nineteenth-century shoemaker would have used. Today's tradesmen make shoes, boots, fire buckets and other leather items, many of which are used or worn by the Old Salem interpretive staff. They make shoes on a "straight last," which was designed to fit both feet. Over time, the leather shoes stretched to fit the contour of the feet.

Tradesmen also make the black leather firebuckets that every Salem household kept on hand in case of fire.

On chilly days, the shop is warmed by a ten-plate cast iron stove that was manufactured in Philadelphia around 1830. Another apparatus that made the shoemaker's work easier on dark days was the water lens, which held four water-filled glass globes around a candle, intensifying the light ten to fifteen times.

The Shultz house and shop complex represents an important architectural shift that occurred in Salem beginning in the 1820s. While earlier houses contained the workshop as well as the living area, at this time tradesmen began to build separate workshops adjacent to their houses. Some, like Samuel Shultz, built a house first and added the shop building later. Some Single Brothers built a small shop first, working and saving money to build a dwelling house and marry. Most shops conformed to a common style, a narrow one or one-and-a-half-story building, with the gable end facing the street.

Architecture Key

Shoe Shop

The House

Samuel Shultz built this frame house around a large central chimney, with a boxed cornice and a steep gabled roof, and with four rooms on each of its two stories.

From 1819 to 1827, Shultz's shoe shop was in the house itself. Porches and additions were built onto the rear of the building over the years, but the street facade of the house has remained largely unchanged.

(Now a private residence)

The Shoemaker Shop

Built in 1827, this building is one of five original shops surviving in Salem. It is compact, with only one story and one room. On the west end of the building there is a free-standing exterior chimney, the only one surviving in Old Salem. The free-standing chimney reduced the danger of fire from the iron stove inside. The many windows provided natural light to work by.

A frame wing was added to the shop between 1885 and 1890, and an additional wing was built five years later. The building functioned as a private residence for many years. The additions were taken down when Old Salem restored the shop in 1978.

(Above)
The form of the Shultz house, with its central chimney, boxed cornice, and gable roof, was common for houses built in Salem from 1815 to 1825. The Shultz Shop, next to the house, has the gable roof of most workshops in Salem.

(Left, top)
A wooden boot hanging on the front of the shop proclaims the trade carried on inside. Such universal signs and symbols were especially helpful in the early days in Salem, when several languages were spoken by townspeople and visitors. The signs also served, as such signs do today, to help people recognize shops and business from a distance.

(Left, bottom)
The tools and products of an early nineteenth-century shoemaker.

The Timothy Vogler Gunsmith Shop

Timothy Vogler, born in 1806, was one of the seven children of Salem gunsmith and blacksmith Christoph Vogler and his wife Anna. Young Timothy attended the Boys' School and in 1819 was apprenticed to his cousin, John Vogler, to learn the important craft and trade of gunsmithing.

In 1824, Timothy left John Vogler's house and moved back into his father's house to learn the blacksmith trade. By this time, Christoph Vogler's health was beginning to fail. Unbeknownst to the church council, he had rented the labor of a free African American man "to carry on the handicraft of a blacksmith." Christoph said that it was his intention to have the blacksmith teach Timothy the trade, as the father was "himself too feeble to teach him." Because of his poor health, Christoph Vogler asked the church council to make him a special exception to their rule of prohibiting congregation members from independently employing African American labor. His petition was denied in February 1825, and he promised to send the African American blacksmith away.

Christoph Vogler died December 11, 1827, and his son Nathaniel was permitted to take over his father's business. Sometime after 1828, Timothy Vogler traveled to Georgia to practice his trade as a journeyman gunsmith. By the spring of 1831, Timothy received permission, with the help of his brother Nathaniel, to return from Georgia to carry on the gunsmith trade in Salem.

Timothy Vogler's gunsmith business grew, and his reputation as a skilled craftsman spread beyond Salem through the nineteenth century. As late as 1878, a master craftsman at age 72, Brother Vogler was still plying his trade in the gunsmith shop. Salem printers L.Y. and E.T. Blum published *A Guide Book of N.W. North Carolina* in 1878. According to the text, "The Vogler and Foltz rifle was well known and highly appreciated by the bold mountain hunters, and those guns have to this day never been surpassed for excellence. Timothy Vogler is yet at his old stand and William Dettmar, who learned the trade with T. Vogler, carries on the Gun and Locksmith business further up town, and fully sustains the well earned reputation of T. Vogler." Timothy Vogler died on January 5, 1896 at the age of 89.

When you visit the Vogler Gunsmith Shop today you will see costumed interpreters working in the trades of gunsmithing, locksmithing, and blacksmithing. During his long career, Timothy Vogler produced rifles, shotguns, door locks, coffee mills, latches, and hinges. Today's craftsmen base their work on many of the surviving artifacts from Vogler's shop, some of which can be seen in MESDA. Each reproduction involves the use of skills ranging from brazing and soldering, to casting and forging. In addition, the tradesmen must work in the areas of engraving, inlay, carving, and gunstock shaping. The gunsmith's trade involves many disciplines, and the tradesmen work with wood, iron, steel, brass, and silver to produce authentic reproductions that are decorative as well as functional.

Architecture Key
The Timothy Vogler House and Gunsmith Shop
909-913 South Main Street. Built 1832 and 1831; restored 1960 & 2001. Lot 98.

Gun Shop

The House

Timothy Vogler built this four-bay, two-story frame house in 1832. The exterior of this house is similar to most built in Salem between 1820 and 1850.

The two end chimneys and balanced placement of windows create an obvious emphasis on symmetry. End chimneys replaced the one large central chimney found in many Salem structures of the mid to late eighteenth century. Vogler and his wife, Charlotte Hamilton, lived in his Gunsmith Shop while the house was constructed.

(Now a private residence)

The Gunsmith Shop

The 1831 Timothy Vogler Gunsmith Shop is the earliest and best documented gunsmith shop remaining in the United States. One of only five surviving shops in Salem, it is a prime example of the importance of trade shops in the community. The structure was originally built with two rooms, as proposed in plans approved by the church council.

The timber-framed building has brick nogging and is built on stone foundations. The exterior siding appears to have been originally unpainted, which, while unusual on the main street, reflects the utilitarian nature of the building and its "remote" location in 1832.

(Above) An 1882 view of the Timothy Vogler House and Gunsmith Shop.

(Left) This c. 1970 image shows the Timothy Vogler Gunsmith Shop prior to restoration.

(Below) The Vogler Gunsmith Shop today without a painted exterior.

St. Philips Church

"Were you a slave
then called? Never
mind . . . For he
who was called in
the Lord as a slave
is a freedman of
the Lord."

1 Corinthians 7:21

Chaplain Clarke,
to the congregation
of St. Philips,
May 21, 1865

In the eighteenth century, white Moravians saw no conflict between keeping Africans and African Americans enslaved and worshiping beside them as spiritual equals. Later, however, attitudes began to change. By the early nineteenth century, a hardening segregation throughout the nation took its toll even on the somewhat tolerant and egalitarian Brethren of Wachovia.

First, contact between white and black Moravians was reduced by requiring African Americans to sit in the back of the church or in the balcony. From 1816, Moravians of African descent were no longer buried in God's Acre, but in the old Strangers' Graveyard at the south end of town. By 1823, when a separate church was built for the African Americans who lived in and around Salem, some of them expressed relief at being able to worship in a place where they would not be constantly treated as second-class members of the church.

In 1822, three Afro Moravians and about fifty other African Americans, most enslaved and owned by the Salem councils, organized their own mission congregation. In 1823, they erected a modest log church near the Strangers' Graveyard, on the south edge of town. Built by the volunteer labor of thirty African American workers, the church was a simple log building measuring 32 by 28 feet. Originally called the "Negro Church" or "African Church," after 1914 it was called St. Philips Church. It is the oldest African American congregation in the country.

In this church, Moravian and non-Moravian African Americans worshiped under the care of a series of white pastors. The Female Missionary Society established a Sunday School in 1827 where African Americans were taught to read and write. This project persisted even after 1831, when the state of North Carolina made it illegal to teach slaves to read or write.

The congregation of St. Philips came from Salem, Waughtown, and an area to the south of Salem that was set aside as the "Negro quarter." By 1860, its attendance had grown so that far more space was needed. The log church was replaced

Squire

Squire, an enslaved African American in Salem, died on July 23, 1844, while he was digging a well near the wool factory built and owned by Francis Fries.

By the time of Squire's death, the Moravian Church no longer purchased enslaved African Americans to rent to members of the congregation, but individual members were permitted to do so if they abided by the 1820 regulations about slaves in Salem. While the Church would not buy Squire and his wife, Brother Fries was free to do so.

Squire was a Baptist, but he and his wife worshipped at the African Moravian Church at the south end of Church Street. This was not unusual; around 70 percent of the congregation was non-Moravian.

A far-sighted businessman, Francis Fries understood the virtues of up-to-date, efficient manufacturing technology. But he could not run his wool mill, and, later his paper and cotton mills, without men to operate the machinery. Enslaved African Americans operated the machines in the factory and worked in the plantation fields. By 1847, seven white workers and sixteen enslaved African Americans were working on Fries's land or in his factory.

Squire, in his forties, was labeled "old" in the Salem minutes, but he was evidently strong and agile enough to be assigned to dig the new well needed for the wool factory. On that fateful summer's day in 1844, he died when the earth at the well site caved in and buried him alive.

Squire was laid to rest in the graveyard near the log church where he had worshipped every Sunday. His gravestone, uncovered by Salem archaeologists in June 1998, records his name, the date of his death, and his age.

in 1861 by a larger brick church, built in the Greek Revival style, with a bell tower and a handsome altar and pews. From its pulpit, on May 21, 1865, Chaplain Clark from the 10th Ohio Cavalry regiment, then occupying Salem, announced that the Civil War was over and that Salem's enslaved population was now free.

In the turbulent days after the Civil War, St. Philips Church offered stability to the community. In its thriving Sunday School, as many as three hundred freed men, women, and children learned to read and write—vital skills for embracing full citizenship in the state and nation.

In 1867, the Society of Friends built a school for African Americans on land donated by the Moravian Church. It was located to the east of Salem on a plantation that would later be called Happy Hill.

An addition to the brick church was built in 1890 to accommodate the growing crowds that came to worship and attend the Sunday School. By 1952, the congregation relocated to Happy Hill, where a new sanctuary was built in 1959. The St. Philips congregation worships today in its fourth location, in the northern part of Winston-Salem.

For a time after the Civil War, the old log church housed a Freedman's Hospital. It was demolished in the early twentieth century. In 1999, a new log building was raised on its original site. The log church now houses the core interpretive exhibit for the St. Philips Complex, which can be visited by purchasing an Old Salem "All-in-One" ticket.

The 1823 African Moravian Church, in a c.1840 lithograph.

"The log church having been for some time already, too small & inconvenient, the erection of the new and larger building . . . was resolved upon and undertaken in reliance upon the help & blessing of the Lord."

Negro Diary, August 24, 1861

7. Salem from 1850 to 1950

The eighteenth century in Salem was a time of beginnings. The mid-nineteenth century in Salem marked the onset of a series of endings. One of the most significant occurred in 1857, when Salem ceased to function as a Moravian congregation town. Almost a century later, in 1950, Old Salem Inc., was established to preserve the legacy of this extraordinary community.

By the 1940s Salem was a busy mercantile district, as shown by this row of Krispy Kreme Doughnut Company delivery vans at the original store location on Main Street.

THE END OF THE CONGREGATION TOWN

In the mid-1850s, the Moravians of Salem confronted major issues in the governance of their town, from questions about the language to be used in official records, to the policies to be used in leasing and selling land. On February 14, 1856, the Salem Congregation Council passed a resolution providing that minutes be written in English rather than German. On November 17, 1856, the Moravian Church Council voted to abolish the lease system that had prohibited people who were not Moravians from owning property in Salem and conducting businesses in their own names. After Salem had become incorporated, the first election of a mayor and eight town commmissioners took place January 5, 1857.

The Moravian theocracy (town governed by the church) was giving way to a separation of the sacred and the secular. Newly elected Mayor Charles Brietz and the Board of Town Commissioners now oversaw municipal affairs. The old lease system would be supplanted by a more conventional land purchase system, and individuals, including non-Moravians, would begin to buy Salem land.

A few years earlier, Salem had given up its role as the central town in the region. When Stokes County was divided in 1849, putting Wachovia in newly created Forsyth County, Salem was the logical site for the county courthouse. The Moravians, however, strongly opposed having Salem become the county seat. They knew from past experience the trouble that Strangers could stir up when they came to town for court sessions and other county business. Instead the Moravians sold 51 acres of land to the county for the site of the new town, which in January 1851 was named Winston for Major Joseph Winston, a hero of the Revolutionary War. Although the Moravians elected to keep as much to themselves as possible to preserve the peace and identity of Salem, some community members anticipated that Winston's proximity would be good for Salem businesses.

THE END OF PACIFISM

Even before the Moravians settled in Wachovia, a 1749 Act of the English Parliament had taken note of certain principles that the Moravians considered essential: "Several of the said Brethren do. . . conscientiously scruple the bearing Arms, or personally serving in any military Capacity, although they are willing and ready to contribute whatever Sums of Money shall be thought a reasonable Compensation for such Service, and which shall be necessary for the Defence and Support of his Majesty's Person and Government." The 1749 Act provided that Moravians would be discharged from military service, provided they paid an assessed sum of money to the government. This was their practice for decades.

In 1831, after years of debate, North Carolina legislators passed a law countermanding such exemption from military service during peacetime for Moravians and other groups in the state, although an annual payment to the state of $2.50 per man would excuse from military service certified members of religious groups whose principles forbade bearing arms in wartime. The Salem congregation decided "it seemed best" under the circumstances to "voluntarily organize" eligible men "into a special company in uniform with rules and regulations for their conduct." In January 1831, the Salem Light Infantry Company, the first Salem peacetime Free Company, was organized and armed with guns furnished by the state.

Not all Moravians condoned the decision. Brother Francis Fries wrote to one of his children on July 30, 1831, "Now in regard to our dear Salem, it is in many ways going to extremes...some for Temperance Society...others have become quite military...Only time will clear it up...an old man such as I am will not care for it...."

During the Civil War, some Moravian men from Salem served in the army of the Confederacy. On June 17, 1861, nearly a month after North Carolina seceded from the Union, the Forsyth Rifles and the Forsyth Grays left Salem for Danville, Virginia. These two companies of volunteers included fifteen members of the Salem congregation and ten men whose parents were members of the Salem congregation. Young men from Bethania and Bethabara joined a third company of Forsyth volunteers departing for Danville on June 24, and during the course of the war, other companies would follow. The Moravians also provided three military bands, commending all to the care of "the God of Battles."

The Moravians had worried that the Civil War would cause a decline in numbers at the Girls' Boarding School. Enrollment actually soared when anxious southern families entrusted their daughters to the school, believing that they would be safer in Salem than at home. When the

dormitories overflowed, many students began boarding with Salem families, and when the Moravians ran out of beds they simply required each girl to bring her own. In 1864 there were 320 students at the boarding school, 149 of whom came from states other than North Carolina.

THE END OF SLAVERY

The Civil War also brought an end to slavery, which had a uniquely convoluted history in Salem. In 1820 the church council had forbidden the Moravians to bring African Americans into Salem as apprentices or skilled workers in any of the trades or crafts. Such workers would threaten the livelihood of the Moravian Brothers and Sisters, it was feared. The 1820 regulation was based on "the conviction that

Main Street in Salem c. 1866 (above), and as it has been restored in the 1990s (below).

91

Salem from 1850 to 1950

trades and handwork in Salem ought to be continued by residents of the town."

Enslaved African Americans could work as "casual laborers" at menial jobs, but even then, special permission had to be granted by the town boards to use slave labor for help in Salem family homes. The householder had to post a bond "double the value of the slave, if he owns him or the double amount of annual rent, if he hires him." Congregation members who lived on farms near Salem were bound through their agreements with the congregation "not to retain in their service any slave who endangers the welfare or the good customs of the town." The Brethren also did not want to jeopardize the work ethic of young Moravians by having others do work in their stead.

As the war ended and African Americans won their freedom, the Moravians had to address such issues as housing and fair wages for hired labor. By January 1867, African American Moravians sought autonomy and freedom within the church, asking permission to have their church services and affairs "as much as possible in their own hands." In that same year, the Moravians gave the land and the Quakers provided the funds to build the first school in this area for African Americans on present-day Happy Hill.

By 1870 the African American Moravian congregation's official ties with the Salem congregation were severed at the request of the Salem Board of Elders. The Provincial Elders Conference then temporarily placed services, but not sacraments, in the hands of three Elders within the congregation until a minister could be found.

Many African Americans in Wachovia continued to work for wages as free men, women, and children in the households and on the farms of their former enslavers. In 1872, they were first permitted to purchase lots on the old Schuman farm that came to be known as Happy Hill. Brother Ned Lemly was the first freedman to purchase a lot in the new settlement. The year 1873 saw the integration of the teaching staff of the Negro Church Sunday School, where there were now four white and three black teachers.

ONE ECONOMIC ERA ENDS AND ANOTHER BEGINS

Reconstruction ended the widespread growth and economic prosperity Salem had enjoyed. After the war, the Bank of Cape Fear went under with the collapse of the Confederate treasury. Salem businesses that had funds and stock tied up in the bank faced ruin along with the bank. John Vogler's venerable silverware, jewelry, and clock repair business, carried on by his son Elias, was virtually wiped out by the bank's collapse, although it was later revived by William T. Vogler, cousin of Elias.

Although by the mid-1870s some Salem merchants had rebuilt or expanded their businesses, Reconstruction brought an end to Salem's domination as the trade and business center of the region. Most of the commercial growth in the area was now taking place in Winston, particularly in the tobacco industry. The young Hanes brothers established a tobacco factory in Winston in 1872. In October 1884, young Richard Joshua Reynolds came to Winston, paid $388.50 for a lot on Chestnut Street, built a two-story tobacco factory, and launched an empire. Salem merchant Edward Belo helped to found and fund the North Western North Carolina Railroad Company, which brought rail service into Winston in July 1873.

With the consolidation of Salem and Winston into one city in 1913, Salem struggled to hold onto its historic identity. By the middle of the twentieth century the city of Winston-Salem was thriving, but historic Salem was living through a period of decline. Over the years, most of its buildings had been altered in appearance and function. The Moravian Church maintained ownership of many key buildings, now used as offices or private dwellings. By the late 1940s, however, Salem's once beautiful, sedate main street was choked with traffic flowing north and south through the city. Many of its historic buildings, so carefully planned and erected, had fallen into disrepair. Urban growth threatened to obliterate the structures that held so much history.

SALEM'S NEW CENTURY

In the 1930s and 1940s, concerned citizens, including some Moravian families, set to work to restore individual dwellings in Salem. The 1768 Fourth House was rescued. The 1793 Ebert-Reich House received a facelift, as did the 1815 Blum House and the Girls' Boarding School wash house, c. 1817. The 1819 John Vogler House was restored, as were the 1831 Kuhln House and the 1844 Siewers House. Individuals joined with church, city, and county officials to explore ways of saving Salem and sustaining the rich legacy of its history.

The Wachovia Historical Society, founded in 1895, played an important part in this process. The society had its roots in the Young Men's Missionary Society, which had opened the first museum in Salem to display natural "curiosities" sent by Moravian missionaries from around the world. The Wachovia Historical Society collected and preserved many examples of early Moravian tools, ceramics, furniture, and works of art, which it displayed in a museum in the Boys' School beginning in 1897. It also purchased the 1784 Salem Tavern and restored it in 1944.

In October 1947, the Citizens Committee for the Preservation of Historic Salem was established to study the feasibility of preserving Salem. In December 1948, the city of Winston-Salem created an historic district in the area around Old Salem. It was only the fifth such locally zoned historic district in the country, and the first in the state.

On March 30, 1950, Old Salem Inc., was officially established as a nonprofit organization to acquire and preserve or

restore "the historical monuments, buildings, sites, locations, areas and/or objects" located in Forsyth County, North Carolina. In the spirit of the first years in Wachovia, many people would now work together to bring renewed life to Salem.

OLD SALEM
TODAY AND TOMORROW

In the half century since its establishment, Old Salem has had the distinction of being declared the first National Historic Landmark District in the state of North Carolina. As of 1999, the boundaries of the district have been extended twice and now encompass over eighty-five acres and more than one hundred historic structures. Numerous gardens, orchards, meadows, and even a stream have been reconstructed or restored, creating an historically accurate landscape setting.

In 1965, Old Salem expanded its mission with the opening of the Museum of Early Southern Decorative Arts (MESDA). In 1997 the Frank L. Horton Museum Center was dedicated. It now houses MESDA, the Toy Museum, the Children's Museum, and the Library and Research Center.

Today Old Salem is a major national visitor attraction, an active partner in the museum and historic preservation community, and a respected research center for the study of southern material culture and Moravian history.

A 1940s super-market (above) at the south end of Old Salem was transformed in 1965 into the Museum of Early Southern Decorative Arts. In 1996, the building was enlarged and rededicated in 1997 as the Frank L. Horton Museum Center.

8. *The Frank L. Horton Museum Center*

At the Horton Center, dedicated in 1997, history and culture come alive in ways that appeal to every visitor. The Museum of Early Southern Decorative Arts (MESDA), which opened in 1965, forms the core of the Horton Center. Visitors can view the finest of southern decorative arts from Maryland to Georgia, and from the Carolinas westward to Kentucky and Tennessee. The Old Salem Toy Museum, one of the most important in the country, exhibits more than 1,200 antique toys representing over 1,700 years of toymaking history. Hands-on activities at the Children's Museum make learning about the past fun for children of all ages.

MESDA

The Museum of Early Southern Decorative Arts, called MESDA for short, opened in 1965. It grew from the vision of Frank L. Horton and his mother, Theo Taliaferro, who saw a need to preserve, document, exhibit, and interpret the decorative arts of the early South. Frank Horton began to dream about this unique museum in 1949 when he learned that a distinguished museum curator had contended, "Little of artistic merit was produced south of Baltimore." Like many other Southerners, he and his mother knew otherwise, and they began to focus on collecting southern decorative arts. They accumulated the

best southern furniture, paintings, and silver that they could find, as well as textiles, ceramics, and other metalwork. In addition, Mr. Horton salvaged architectural interiors from eighteenth- and early nineteenth-century houses that were threatened with demolition.

When a grocery store on the edge of Old Salem became vacant in the early 1960s, Mr. Horton remodeled it as a museum, installing domestic interiors and filling them with furnishings from the appropriate region and time period. Now, as you tour MESDA's thirty rooms, you are immersed in the beauty and fine craftsmanship that characterize the best of southern decorative arts.

Part of Frank Horton's vision was to research and unearth the names of anonymous southern artisans and provide a sound basis for interpreting MESDA's collections. The MESDA–Old Salem Research Center can document over 70,000 southern artists, artisans, and craftsmen and more than 27,000 southern-made objects. It is the only center in the world dedicated to the study of southern decorative arts.

MESDA shares its knowledge through special classes, lectures, and conferences on decorative arts, as well as a graduate-level summer institute each year. In addition, MESDA publishes a scholarly journal and a book series that present new research on specific aspects of southern decorative arts.

Earthenware lion, attributed to potter Solomon Bell, Winchester, Virginia, c. 1840.

THE THREE REGIONS
OF THE SOUTH

From folk art to fine art, encompassing furniture, paintings, ceramics, textiles, and metalwork, MESDA offers visitors a wide range of southern artistry and craftsmanship from the 1670s through the early nineteenth century. Then as now, a rich cultural diversity characterized southern lifestyles, as the MESDA period rooms show.

In the Chesapeake Bay and Tidewater area of Maryland and eastern Virginia and North Carolina, planters who had become wealthy through the tobacco trade filled their houses with simple yet elegant furniture in the latest British style.

Farther south along the coast, in the Lowcountry of South Carolina and Georgia, Charleston reigned as one of the colonies' largest and busiest port cities. Charleston artisans' elegant furniture and silver drew on the rich cultural mix in the city—British, French, and German style, among others.

The Backcountry is the term used to describe the region stretching from the Shenandoah Valley in Virginia to the Carolinas and Georgia, and north to Tennessee and Kentucky. Settled by a variety of ethnic groups, including Germans and Scotch-Irish, and isolated by the rugged terrain, Backcountry communities developed unique regional characteristics. The people of the Backcountry lacked the wealth of their neighbors on the coast, but their furniture, pottery, and metalwork reflect a strong sense of beauty and pride in craftsmanship.

As you tour MESDA, you will visit rooms that represent these three regions and reveal how the styles of each evolved

(Above)
Silver coffeepot,
1750-1760, from the
shop of Alexander
Petrie, Charleston,
South Carolina, who
is thought to have
used the skills of
Abraham, an
enslaved craftsman.

(Left)
Mrs. Samuel
Prioleau, pastel
drawing by
Henrietta Johnston,
Charleston,
South Carolina,
1715. Henrietta
Johnston is the
first professional
woman artist
known in
North America.

The Frank L. Horton Museum Center

*The Piedmont
Room from
Guilford County,
North Carolina,
c. 1766.*

*Dressing table
made in Norfolk,
Virginia,
1750-1765*

over time, between 1670 and 1820. You will see how, in Virginia, the massive turned oak furniture of the seventeenth-century great hall gave way to the "neat and plain" style of the mid-eighteenth century, to be superseded by the neoclassical style of the early nineteenth century. In the Lowcountry, the ornately carved rococo paneling and furniture of the mid-eighteenth century gave way to a lighter, still elegant style. You will be able to compare the heavy, Germanic furniture and the decorated ceramics of the Carolina piedmont with fancifully inlaid Kentucky furniture.

MESDA can be visited by purchasing the Old Salem "All-in-One" ticket.

96

THE OLD SALEM CHILDREN'S MUSEUM

At the Children's Museum, hands-on activities encourage young people to experience what life in Salem was like in the early days. Dressed in Moravian clothing, they can work at a joiner's bench, putting together a box with dovetails or assembling a chair puzzle. They can pretend to cook over an open fire in a scaled-down model of the Miksch House, or make picture profiles using a technique similar to the one silversmith John Vogler used in the 1840s.

Playing with old-fashioned toys such as cloth dolls, hobbyhorses, and blocks sparks the imagination while making history fun. Activities such as the gravity-activated marble run and "touch boxes" filled with natural materials teach children about science, too. Oriented to children between the ages of four and nine, the activities can still be enjoyed by people of all ages.

The Children's Museum regularly offers activities such as puppet shows and special classes. Admission is charged. Membership in the Kater Klub (named after an imaginary Salem cat, Herr Kater), gives children and the adults with them free admission and advance notice of holiday events.

THE OLD SALEM TOY MUSEUM

The Toy Museum is a treasure chest of more than 1200 antique European and American toys exhibiting playthings that people have enjoyed for nearly two thousand years.

Here you can see toys that archaeologists discovered in the River Thames in London—miniature bronze firearms from 1585 to 1610, and a lead die dating back to 225 A.D. You can see toys Moravian children played with in the nineteenth and twentieth centuries. You can find a variety of German toys—ships and marbles, games and puzzles, cars and trains. You can see dolls from the seventeenth century through the earliest twentieth century. You can look at teddy bears and puppets, doll houses and toy zoos, and toys made of porcelain, silver or cast iron. You can discover the "Humpty Dumpty Circus," the largest public collection of this magical circus to be crafted by German-American toy master Albert Schoenhut.

The museum was established by Thomas A. Gray, an Old Salem Trustee, and his mother, Anne P. Gray, who loved and collected toys for many years, and used their knowledge to build the Toy Museum around Old Salem's collection of nineteenth and early twentieth century toys.

*(Left)
Assembling a chair puzzle in the Old Salem Children's Museum.*

*(Above)
Images from the Old Salem Toy Museum, clockwise from top: one of the displays in the circus room; a camel pull toy, 1890, Germany; and a tin toy car, c. 1906, Germany, in front of a wood-and-ink building, c. 1904, Germany.*

9. *Street Guide to Buildings in Old Salem*

Use this section as a guide to the architecture you see around you as you stroll through Old Salem. It describes all buildings in the historic district, the architectural periods and features they represent, and some of their more interesting inhabitants.

Structures on north-south streets are given first: Main Street, Church Street, Salt Street, and Factory Row, with houses listed from north to south. The cross streets follow: Academy Street, West Street, Blum Street, and Walnut Street, with houses listed from east to west.

The lot numbers given (not to be confused with the Lot used to make decisions) come from the original numbering system used when Salem was first planned. They are still used for research purposes.

Unlike other living-history museums, Old Salem is also part of a modern neighborhood, sharing the historic district with the Moravian Church, Salem Academy and College, and many private residents. Here people work, live, study, and worship in an atmosphere that respects and protects the history of this place. Please feel free to visit Old Salem exhibit buildings, the gardens, the shops, and the public buildings, while respecting the privacy of the other homes and offices.

Main Street

The Coffee Pot
Lot 45

The Coffee Pot, one of Winston-Salem's best-known landmarks, was originally located two blocks to the north. It was made in 1858 as a shop sign by tinsmiths Julius and Samuel Mickey. When the shop site was claimed about 1960 by Interstate 40 (now Business 40), it was moved to its current location.

313 South Main Street
Tilla Stockton House c. 1875
Lot 83

This one-and-a-half story Victorian house has been described as a cottage with Tuscan villa characteristics. Italianate features include the windows above and on each side of the double-leaf door, the arched porch roof supports, the tall four-over four windows, and the decorative carved moldings on the woodwork. Miss Tilla Stockton was a music teacher who gave lessons in her home and at Salem College.

319 South Main Street
Peter Fetter House c. 1840
Lot 83

Peter Fetter, a chairmaker, received permission to set up a chairmaking business in Salem in 1839. He built this frame house around 1840 on a subdivision of lot 83, and over the years also built shop buildings and a stable on the same site.

A later owner converted the house into a duplex, removing the front and back porches, changing the windows, adding an ell at the back of the house, and building side porches over the new entrances. Similar multifamily dwellings were common in Salem at the beginning of the twentieth century, when it was a densely populated urban area.

327 South Main Street
Welfare House c. 1855
Lot 43

Because of subdivisions to lot 43 over the years, the history of this house is unclear. Alanson Welfare, a gunsmith, watchmaker, and locksmith, purchased the north half of lot 43 in 1855 and may have built the house at that time.

331 South Main Street
Charles Pfohl House c. 1905
Lot 43

A late addition to the Main Street landscape, the Pfohl House, with its many gables, varied roof lines, tall chimneys, and decorative shingles, is an interesting example of an early twentieth-century house.

403 South Main Street
Dr. Fred Pfohl House 1915
Lot 42

Dr. Pfohl had a private practice in this house and also served as the Salem Academy and College physician from 1917 to 1938. His two-story, four-bay house was built on a raised lot, surrounded by masonry walls. It was built with an office suite on the north side, reflecting the early Salem practice of combining workplace and residence.

411 South Main Street
Charles Cooper Shop c. 1834, reconstructed 1979
Lot 41

The Cooper Shop was built around 1834 by Charles Cooper, a furniture maker and house painter. It was reconstructed by Old Salem using archaeological and archival evidence, including historic photographs. It represents the custom of building a separate shop building begun in the 1820s. Cooper's house, which has not been reconstructed, was located to the north of the shop.

416 South Main Street
Owen House c. 1920
Lot 47

This one-and-a-half-story brick bungalow stands on the lot once occupied by the blacksmith's house and shop, which were built in 1768 by George Schmidt. The blacksmith's shop, like the potter's, was located on the edge of town to avoid the risk of fire.

421 South Main Street
Hall House 1827 with 1843 alterations, rest. 1976
Lot 40

This two-story, five-bay frame house is a fine example of a combination shop and residence in Salem. Its two entry doors have a shared stoop. From 1841 James Hall used the house as a bakery, bake shop, and residence. In that year he dug a new cellar to house a bake room with an oven, and in 1843 he built a back porch with a new kitchen. The house has been restored to its 1843 configuration.

427 South Main Street
Beitel–Van Vleck House 1841,
reconstructed 1976
Lot 39

This house was built by tailor Edward Beitel around an existing shop building. It is typical of Salem dwellings in the 1840s: a one-and-a-half-story, five-bay frame house, with a wood-shingled roof. The house was bought in 1847 by Christina Van Vleck, the widow of Charles Van Vleck. The lane to the north of the house, called Maiden Lane, was named for the Van Vlecks' daughters, "Miss Amy" and "Miss Lou," who were instructors at Salem College.

The Coffee Pot was once a shop sign for tinsmiths Julius and Samuel Mickey.

428 South Main Street
Shaffner House 1874
Lot 48

This fine example of the Second Empire style reflects the growing wealth in Salem in the 1870s. It was designed by Elias A. Vogler, son of silversmith John Vogler, for physician John Francis Shaffner and his wife, Caroline Fries, who was Elias' niece. Dr. Shaftner, a protégé of Francis Fries, was a leader in Salem's development as an industrial center in the late nineteenth century. Caroline was the daughter of Lisetta Vogler and Francis Fries. The house was part of a complex of buildings, including Dr. Shaffner's drugstore, an ice house, and a smokehouse/kitchen. It features a pressed-brick facade with richly ornamented pediments over the windows, decorative brick pilasters and brackets, round arched dormer windows, and a scalloped slate mansard roof.

Lot 48 was the site of the 1771 church-owned pottery, first operated by Gottfried Aust and maintained by a series of potters until 1843.

433 South Main Street
Stockton House 1905
Lots 37, 38

A wide porch shades the tracery and bevelled glass inserts of the doorway and windows on this Colonial Revival house. Distinctive windows and roof details accentuate the central entrance. It stands on the site of an 1826 saddler's shop and house, which in 1831 was converted into a second community store, run by Theodor Pfohl.

434 South Main Street
Fifth House 1767, reconstructed 1975
Lot 49

This row of houses represents the earliest houses built in Salem, using the *fachwerk,* or half-timbering technique brought from Germany by the first builders. Of the four standing houses in this row, only the second from the north, the Fourth House, is original. The rest have been reconstructed using archaeological evidence and early plans in the Moravian Church Archives.

First used to house day laborers, the Fifth House was occupied by a cabinetmaker in 1772 and was used by the potters Gottfried Aust and Rudolf Christ as an extension of the pottery site to the north. A pottery kiln was built in the back yard at one time.

The 1766
First House
(reconstructed)
shows the
fachwork, *or*
half-timbering,
technique familiar
to the early
Moravians, many
of whom were
German-born.

438 South Main Street
Fourth House 1768, restored 1966
Lot 50

The oldest surviving building in Salem, the Fourth House has what is known as a *Flurkuchenhaus* (hall-kitchen house) plan, with three rooms around a central chimney. This was a common floor plan in Salem until the early nineteenth century. Like the Third and Fifth houses, it has an asymmetrical facade, half-timbered walls filled with brick, and a steep tile roof with a kick eave. In the late 1880s, the Fourth House was moved back from the street and raised several feet to accommodate the grading of Main Street for the trolley line. In 1936 the Society of Colonial Dames purchased the house and partially restored it. Old Salem leased the house in 1966 and restored it to its 1768 appearance.

440 South Main Street
Third House 1767, reconstructed 1969
Lot 51

The Third House was constructed along the same plan as its neighbors, but with a cellar under the whole house that could be used as a weaver's or cabinetmaker's shop. During the American Revolution, the cellar served as an infirmary for sick soldiers. In 1847, a room in this house was used to house the Young Men's Missionary Society "museum," a collection of zoological and botanical specimens and other "curiosities" that had been donated by Moravian missionaries in the course of their work in foreign countries. The first museum in North Carolina, it was the precursor of the Wachovia Historical Society.

446 South Main Street
First House 1766, reconstructed 1969
Lot 52

The building of the First House was a momentous event in Salem; eighteen Brethren gathered to celebrate the laying of the cornerstone on June 6, 1766. Unlike its neighbors, the half-timbering of the First House was filled with wattle and daub and covered with plaster. In the first years it housed a family and also had a Saal, or room for worship, that was used until the Gemein Haus was built in 1771. In the eighteenth century some of its most notable occupants were Dr. Jacob Bonn, the first physician in Salem, and his successor Samuel Benjamin Vierling and his family.

The lot south of the First House is the site of the Second House, the only of the "first houses" to have two stories. It has not been reconstructed due to inadequate documentary evidence.

455 South Main Street
Edward Belo House 1849
Lots 35, 36

This imposing structure was built by Edward Belo. A prominent cabinetmaker and owner of an iron foundry, Belo was one of the leaders in Salem's growth as an industrial center after the Civil War. The house is considered one of the best examples of Greek Revival style in North Carolina. Its center frame section is flanked by two brick structures, three stories high. The first floor housed a store; the upper floors of the south end served as living quarters for Belo, his wife Amanda Fries (sister of industrialist Francis Fries), and their seven children. In 1859 a third story was built on the center frame section, and Corinthian columns were added to the Main Street facade. One of the house's most impressive features is its decorative ironwork, cast in Belo's foundry: fencing, hitching posts, statues of a lion and two dogs, and the grillwork on the Main Street facade and the Bank Street portico.

In 1960 the house was converted into apartments for elderly Moravian church members who were living in the Single Brothers' House (then known as the Widows' House). This allowed the Single Brothers' House to be restored.

500 South Main Street
Cape Fear Bank 1847
Lot 54

In 1846, when the church business board decided to allow the Cape Fear Bank of Wilmington to establish a branch in Salem, no available building was considered suitable to house a bank. The Collegium chose to build a two-story brick house with a fireproof vault. Its two entrances, one for the manager's living quarters and one for the business, share a common stoop. The house was built using the common bond bricklaying method, not the Flemish bond of earlier buildings such as the Vorsteher's House across the street.

The garden behind the house is an interpretation of an 1840s Salem family garden.

501 South Main Street
Vorsteher's House 1797
Lot 34

This house was the residence of the Vorsteher, or business manager, of Salem. The first house to be built by a non-Moravian builder, William Craig, it had two unusual features: an A-shaped hood over the Main Street entrance, and a brick cantilever, or course of brick, delineating the coved, plastered cornice. The ground floor walls were stuccoed, and the walls above were brick, laid in Flemish bond. The tile roof was replaced with shingles in 1859.

The doorway was probably recessed in 1899 to correct a problem caused by the lowering of the street level when the trolley was introduced in 1890.

508 South Main Street
John Henry Leinbach House 1822, restored 1962
Lot 55

John Henry Leinbach, a shoemaker, and his wife Elizabeth built this house in 1822. His shop was in the house, but it did not have a separate entrance. The shop did have four windows, two facing the street and two on the north side, so that he would have enough light to work. With its interior end chimneys and central hall plan, this house departs from the early Germanic central-chimney house style used in Salem.

Leinbach kept a detailed diary of his gardening, farming, and work activities. This has guided the interpretation of the family garden behind the house, with its earth and stone terraces. John Henry and Elizabeth's son Henry was a prominent early photographer in Salem; in 1868 he built a daguerreotype gallery on the north end of the house. This was removed when the house was restored.

511 South Main Street
Herbst House 1821
Lot 33

This house, built by saddlemaker Heinrich Herbst, was the first example of a porch-over-sidewalk house built in Salem. (See the Butner House, next door.) It was originally built directly on the sidewalk with a full cellar at street level, where a shop was located for a time. In 1890 the house was moved back from the sidewalk and underwent alterations to the chimneys, windows, and doorway. The house's second owner, Charles Brietz, was the first mayor of Salem.

After extensive archaeology and research, the building has been moved back to its original location on the street and restored to its 1820s appearance, including the porch over the sidewalk and basement level. The lower level has been restored, but the upper floors were rehabilitated for modern uses. Currently, the building houses the Friends of Old Salem Hospitality Center, and office space.

516 South Main Street
Levering House 1820, reconstructed 1972
Lot 56

Reconstructed to its 1820 configuration, this house is similar to the Leinbach House to the north but exhibits some older features, primarily the center chimney and the three-room layout around it. The garden behind the house was terraced to make best use of the sloped lot; it now has vegetable and flower beds and a grape arbor, reflecting the plants that would have been grown in a typical 1820s Salem garden.

517 South Main Street
Butner House and Shop 1828 and 1825, house restored 1961, shop reconstucted 1965
Lot 32

The two-story porch-over-sidewalk house was common in Salem by the late nineteenth century; the Butner House, built by hatmaker Adam Butner, is the only example to have survived. The frame, gable-end shop is typical of the shop buildings in

the 1820s and 1830s. The house, on the other hand, has several formal decorative features that set it apart from Moravian architecture of the time, including the Doric columns on the two-story porch, the elaborate cornice, the decorative carving on the porch stairs, and the pedimented gables.

After Salem ceased to function as a congregation town in 1856, the Butner House was bought by the town to house the civil government. It was the site of the "Town Hall and Watch House" until another was built a few years later. It was restored in 1961.

520 South Main Street
Schroeter House 1805 and 1832, reconstructed in 1968
Lot 57

Johann Gottlob Schroeter, a tailor, had this house built using materials from a laundry building that was being torn down behind the Gemein Haus (now the site of Main Hall). Schroeter's use of salvaged materials may be responsible for the original house's low roof line. After Schroeter's death in 1832, the next owner, tobacconist Benjamin Warner, added the shop on the south end of the building. The house has been reconstructed to its 1832 appearance, with the shop addition.

529 South Main Street
Winkler Bakery 1800, restored 1967–68
Lot 31
An Old Salem exhibit building; see p. 75.

532 S. Main Street
Miksch House and Manufactory 1771, restored 1960
Lot 59
An Old Salem exhibit building; see p. 43.

600 South Main Street
Single Brothers' House 1769 and 1786, restored 1964
Lot 62
An Old Salem exhibit building; see p. 41.

101

A wooden rifle hangs next to the doorway to the shop of the 1797 Christoph Vogler House, indicating his trade as a gunsmith.

and doors. The gable ends of the building are decorated with brick laid in elaborate herringbone patterns. On the south side, Krause spelled out his initials, IGK, in contrasting brick ("I" is used in place of "J"). On the facade of the building, between the doorways, he spelled out the letter W, possibly for Vogler. Christoph Vogler's trade is indicated by the gun that hangs by the door to the shop.

In the mid-1950s, Old Salem restored the house to its original appearance, removing a second story and a two-story front porch added in the late nineteenth century.

712–714 South Main Street
Lot 66
Shultz House and Shoemaker Shop
1819 and 1827; house restored 1961,
shop restored 1978
The Shultz Shoe Shop is an Old Salem exhibit building; the house is a private residence.
See p. 85.

715 South Main Street
Nathaniel Shober Siewers House 1871–1875
Lot 26
This house was one of the first built in Salem after the Civil War. It replaced a central-chimney log house built in 1788 by Philip Transou. The two-story, three-bay facade is distinguished from its neighbors by a hipped roof with projecting eaves and a wide plain cornice, large six-over-six sash windows, and the geometric latticework of its front porch.

Dr. Nathaniel Siewers and his wife, Eleanor de Schweinitz, later built the Gothic Revival mansion, Cedarhyrst, on Church Street; see p. 103.

723 South Main Street
Joshua Boner House 1844
Lot 25
In 1844 Joshua Boner received permission to tear down an old log house on lot 25 and build a large two-story frame house with interior end chimney on a fieldstone foundation. He operated a general store out of the northern front room. Its separate double-door entrance is interesting because it is out of proportion to the entrance to his living quarters.

724 South Main Street
Blum House, now J. Blum: Printer and Merchant
1815, enlarged 1854, restored 1995
Lot 67
John Christian Blum built this house in 1815 as a one-and-a-half story frame structure with end chimneys. At the time he was the agent for the Cape Fear Bank, and the north room, with its separate entrance, served as the banking room. Blum made his mark in Salem as a printer of Salem's first newspapers, however, and his printing press is now displayed here. In 1854 one of Blum's sons added the second story to the house and an external chimney to the north. In keeping with its nineteenth-century use as a print shop and bookshop, the Blum House is now a gift shop.

612–614 South Main Street
Elias Vogler Store; Moravian Book & Gift Shop
1867, altered 1930s
Lot 62
This late-1930s Colonial Revival storefront began life as an 1867 Italianate Victorian designed by Elias A. Vogler. From the original configuration some features still remain, such as the pilasters on the facade of the building, and the corbelled brick cornice on the north and south sides, behind the gabled roof line.

Vogler was a prominent businessman, architect, artist and map maker. He was a member of the first Board of Commissioners and was the second mayor of Salem. He operated a store in this building, but he went into bankruptcy in the 1870s. The Moravian Church currently operates a book and gift shop here.

Salem Square, facing Main Street
Market-Firehouse 1803, reconstructed 1955
An Old Salem exhibit building; see p. 27.

626 South Main Street
Community Store; T. Bagge: Merchant 1775,
restored 1954
Lot 63
An Old Salem exhibit building and museum store;
see p. 51.

700 South Main Street
John Vogler House 1819, restored 1954
Lot 64
An Old Salem exhibit building; see p. 83.

710 South Main Street
Christoph Vogler House 1797, restored c. 1955
Lot 65
Gunsmith Christoph Vogler had this house built by master mason and builder Johann Gottlob Krause, whose striking brickwork embellishes many Salem buildings. It features dark, glazed headers, a molded brick watercourse around the base of the first story, and rubbed brick in the arches over the windows

The 1824 Traugott Leinbach House, in an 1890s photograph.

731 South Main Street
Ebert-Reich House 1793, alterations made in 1801 and 1843; renovated 1938
Lot 24

This house began life as a one-and-a-half-story log house and was expanded over the course of the nineteenth century. It was built by Johann Ebert, a wood turner who was asked to leave Salem in 1796. It was subsequently occupied by Johann Christoph Reich, a coppersmith, who sheathed it in weatherboarding in 1801. Reich built a house on Church Street in 1823, but died before it was finished.

736 South Main Street
Salem Tavern Restaurant 1816, restored 1968
Lot 68

This two-story, five-bay building with front porch, called the "boarding house," was built in 1816 to provide more lodging for visitors, or Strangers, staying at the Salem Tavern. In 1832 a dining hall annex was built connecting the boarding house and the brick tavern, and sometime after 1838 a continuous two-story front porch was added to this tavern complex (see photo, p. 61).

The dining hall annex had been removed by 1897. In 1968 the former boarding house was restored to its 1816 exterior appearance and adapted for use as a restaurant.

800 South Main Street
Salem Tavern 1785, restored 1956
Lot 68

An Old Salem exhibit building; see p. 61.

803 South Main Street
Augustus Zevely House,
now Augustus Zevely Inn 1844, restored 1994
Lot 23

In 1844 David Blum built this large two-story brick house with a one-story ell in the back. He subsequently sold it to Dr. Augustus Zevely. The house is a late example of the house-and-shop combination with two entry doors, each with separate stoop. Its common bond brickwork and corbelled brick cornice are typical of 1840s architecture in Salem. The ell along Blum Street was raised from one story to two in 1858.

In the late 1840s and 1850s Dr. Zevely took in guests who could not find lodging in the Salem Tavern across the street. Consistent with this early use, the Zevely House now is a bed-and-breakfast inn.

807 South Main Street
Traugott Leinbach House 1824, reconstructed 1975
Lot 22

Traugott Leinbach was a silversmith and pioneer daguerrean. He built this one-and-a-half-story house in 1824 with separate entrances to his shop and living quarters. The family entry has a fanlight above the door.

In the 1850s Leinbach built a three-story addition to the north of the house, which abutted an addition made by Augustus Zevely to his house (see photo). By 1912, the Leinbach House had been torn down and lot 22 was subdivided. The house was reconstructed in 1975.

823 South Main Street
Jacob Siewers House 1845, restored 1971
Lot 21

This is a fine example of the Greek Revival style in Salem, with its low gable roof and its porch with Tuscan columns surmounted by a deck with railing. It boasts fine woodworking details such as windows with raised panels, set within molded surrounds with corner blocks. The foundation is stuccoed and painted to imitate cut stone blocks. The exterior end chimneys have stepped shoulders, an early example of this practice in Salem.

832 South Main Street
John Siewers House 1844
Lot 102

This house site was subdivided from the Salem Tavern property in 1839. Cabinetmaker John Siewers, brother of Jacob, built this one-and-a-half-story house on a one-story brick foundation. It has a fine pedimented portico with paired columns, common-bond brickwork, and a corbelled brick cornice, like those seen on other buildings built in the 1840s.

This house has retained a high degree of its architectural integrity, leading it to be called "a preservation, not a restoration." The garden next to the house, which is maintained by the owner, is a carefully researched interpretation of an 1850s pleasure garden.

103

Old Salem Street Guide

Cedarhyrst, the imposing Gothic Revival mansion overlooking God's Acre.

901 South Main Street
Kuehln House 1831
Lot 97

This two-story brick house was built in 1831 as a house and apothecary for Dr. David Kuehln, who came to Salem in 1818. It represents an early use of common bond brickwork. The north chimney is a partial external chimney, but the southern chimney is internal, located between the apothecary and house areas. While most in-house work spaces were in north front rooms, Dr. Kuehln's apothecary was in the south end of the house; you can see the bricked-in apothecary doorway.

909–913 South Main Street
Timothy Vogler House and Shop
1832 and 1831, house restored 1960
Lot 98

Shop is an Old Salem exhibit building; see p. 87.

After the Single Brothers' House was closed in 1823, a Single Brother often established himself as an independent artisan by first building a workshop. There he would live and work, saving money to build a larger, separate dwelling. This was the case with gunsmith Timothy Vogler, the son of Christoph and cousin of John Vogler. He built his shop in 1831 and the house after he married Charlotte Hamilton in 1832.

The four-bay, two-story frame house with interior chimneys was affected by the raising of the street grade for the 1890 trolley line. The one story, gable end shop was raised by laying a brick foundation on top of the original fieldstone foundation.

This block, which was laid out around 1829, has wider lots than the rest of the town, with frontages of 120 rather than 90 feet.

920 South Main Street
Johannes Volz House 1816, restored 1963
Lot 96

When it was built by retired farmer Johannes Volz in 1816, this house lay outside of town and may have been considered a farm or country house. It was the first private residence in Salem to have a front porch running the length of the house. It was built with a central chimney and side hall plan. Under the porch roof, which is supported by Tuscan columns, the facade is sided with flush board sheeting rather than overlapping weatherboards.

The field to the north of the house is used by Old Salem to grow a variety of field crops that would have been grown on farms in the Salem vicinity. The barn behind the Volz House was moved here from Idol's Dam, on the Yadkin River, in the 1960s.

935 South Main Street
Eberhardt House and Shop 1832 and 1833, house restored 1951; workshop reconstructed 1967
Lot 99

This house was the residence and workshop of locksmith Lewis Eberhardt. The house is one of the last in Salem to be built in the central-chimney configuration, with four rooms. Eberhardt's clockmaking shop was located in a lean-to on the north side of the house, which was added in 1833. The separate gable-end workshop building was originally built as Eberhardt's blacksmith shop a year later, in 1834.

924 South Main Street
Frank L. Horton Museum Center 1948, 1996
An Old Salem exhibit building, housing the Museum of Early Southern Decorative Arts (MESDA), the Old Salem Toy Museum, and the Old Salem Children's Museum. See pages 92–95.

The Frank L. Horton Museum Center houses three different museums and galleries. Architecturally speaking, the building reflects the evolution of the historic district in the second half of the twentieth century. It began life as a supermarket in the 1950s. In the 1960s, it was converted into a museum space by Frank L. Horton and his mother, Theo Talliaferro. They had been looking for a space that could house a museum of early southern decorative arts, for which they had been collecting southern antiques for many years, and the store's location in the historic district of Old Salem was ideal. The Museum of Early Southern Decorative Arts opened in 1965. It is the only museum in the world dedicated to collecting and researching decorative arts from the early South. In the late 1980s MESDA added a wing with new period rooms, a gallery, and an auditorium and classroom. In 1996 a major addition to the south of the building, with post-modern classicizing features and a copper dome, more than doubled the exhibit area. The new space has been dedicated to The Old Salem Children's Museum and The Old Salem Toy Museum, established in 2002 by Thomas A. Gray, an Old Salem Trustee, and his mother, Anne P. Gray.

The Covered Bridge 1999
Although not a type of bridge built by the Moravians in Salem, this covered bridge replicates the double-truss timber bridges that were built in North Carolina in the nineteenth century. It was made from timbers that were recycled from such disparate locations as the Savannah, Gerogia, harbor and the Saint Lawrence Seaway, among others. The bridge connects the historic district and the Old Salem Visitor Center. The truss bridge is the only covered bridge built in North Carolina in last hundred years.

Church Street

455 Church Street
Charles Kremer House 1841,
renovation post-1873
Lot 5

While the norm for most houses in Salem was to be located on the street, the Moravian church elders stipulated that the Kremer house should be set back from the street so that it would not damage the allee of "beautiful cedar trees" lining the walk to God's Acre. The original one-and-one-half-story brick house was built by Charles Kremer, a saddler, and his wife Eliza Vierling, the daughter of Dr. Vierling. The Victorian embellishments, including the octagonal bays on the facade and the north end, the elaborately decorated porch, and a dormer window, were probably added after 1873.

459 Church Street
Cedarhyrst 1894
Lot 6

Built for Dr. Nathaniel Siewers, a successful physician, and his wife Eleanor de Schweinitz, Cedarhyrst is a monumental example of the Gothic Revival style in Old Salem. It was designed by New York architect Max Schroff and built by a local construction company, Fogle Brothers. Its asymmetry and distinctive features, such as the cut Indiana limestone walls, pointed arches, slate roof, and stained glass windows, evoke the feeling of a European castle. Like other buildings from the second half of the nineteenth century, it is a major departure from the style and scale of earlier buildings in Salem and demonstrates how Moravians of this period actively sought out new architectural concepts.

463 Church Street
Dr. Samuel Benjamin Vierling House 1802
Lot 7
An Old Salem exhibit building; see p. 77.

500 Church Street
Salem Boys' School 1896
Lot 34

This building was constructed to replace the 1794 Boys' School on Salem Square. Its panelled brickwork and round arches with brownstone keys over paired sash windows, among other features, are typical of the Romanesque Revival style. It is the only surviving school building in this style in Forsyth County. At various times this building housed the Salem Boys' School, the Tinsley Military Academy, Central City Public School, and Salem Academy classes. Since 1931 it has been used as office space by the Moravian Church.

513 Church Street
Steiner House 1823, restored 1969
Lot 9

This house was built for Charles Abraham Steiner, a chairmaker. It has two entrances, one for Steiner's shop and one for the living area. Its six-bay facade is unusually long for houses built in Salem at that

*Main Hall
of Salem Academy
and College,
shortly after
it was built
in 1856.*

time. Many Victorian alterations to the house were removed during restoration, with the exception of the 1874 kitchen wing.

519 Church Street
Bishop's House 1841
Lot 10

In 1840 the Salem congregation decided to turn the Gemein Haus completely over to the Girls' Boarding School and chose this lot, north of the church, for a house for the pastor, who had always lived in the Gemein Haus. The location had the disadvantage, however, of being directly across the street from a horse stable; for this reason it was set back from the street. The straightforward two-story five-bay plan, with common-bond brickwork and Greek Revival portico, is typical of buildings from the mid-nineteenth century, as is the corbelled brick cornice. The house owes its name to the fact that it has housed three bishops of the Moravian Church.

529 Church Street
Home Moravian Church 1800
and later additions.
Lots 11, 12
Open for visitors at specific hours; see p. 69.

601 Church Street
Main Hall 1856,
built on the site of the 1771 Gemein Haus
Lot 13

The Gemein Haus, or Congregation House, was the center of religious life in Salem until Home Church was built in 1800; it was the forum where all administrative matters were dealt with as well. It was built on roughly the same scale as the Single Brothers' House across the square, as a long, two-story structure. The first story was built of fieldstone, and the second was half-timbered; like the SingleBrothers' House, it had a pent eave halfway up the exterior walls. The Vorsteher, or town business manager, lived in the Gemein Haus, as did the minister and his family. It was the home of the Single Sisters as well. The Girls' School held its classes in the building for many years, and by 1840, as the other functions were moved elsewhere, had sole use of the Gemein Haus for its own purposes.

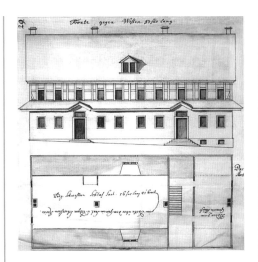

In the 1850s several members of the community addressed the issue of overcrowding in the school, suggesting that the Gemein Haus be replaced with a more spacious modern building. Francis Fries was entrusted with the design and construction of the new edifice. With the help of noted New York architect Alexander Jackson Davis, Fries drew up plans for a dramatic four-story Greek Revival structure.

With its four stories, bold Doric portico and massive cornice and pediment accented with modillon blocks, Main Hall dominates Salem Square. First occupied in March 1856, Main Hall held classrooms, a sleeping hall, dwelling rooms, sick rooms, and storage space. It still is used for classroom and office space by Salem College.

619 Church Street
South Hall (Girls' Boarding School) 1805, restored in 1966
Lot 14

By 1802 the growing reputation of the Girls' School created a demand for boarding students, and the next year work began on a boarding school building. It held classrooms, a dining hall, an attic dormitory for the girls, a sick room, and a storeroom. In 1824 an addition was built on the north end of the building, and in 1837 a clerestory was added to increase ventilation in the dormitory. A number of significant original features from the 1805 structure remain: the hooded stoop entrance, glazed headers set in the Flemish bond pattern, and painted brick on each side of windows and door openings. In the 1930s, a separate building for Salem Academy was built on the back of the campus. South Hall is now used exclusively by Salem College.

627 Church Street
Single Sisters' House 1786, restored 1974
Lot 15
See p. 65.

624 Church Street
Clewell Dormitory 1922
Lot 15

Like a number of twentieth-century Salem College buildings, this dormitory integrates architectural features of eighteenth- and early nineteenth-century

Salem in what has been referred to as the "Moravian Revival" style. This building's two-story design, with a high gable roof, brick relieving arches, dark headers, and arched door openings, harmonizes with the architecture of its older neighbors. Other features, such as the engaged columns with Corinthian capitals supporting an entablature, are more in the spirit of the Colonial Revival.

626 Church Street
Gramley Library 1937, moved 1972
Lot 28

Built in 1937, this building houses the Salem College Library. It was originally located on Salem Square, on the corner of Church and West streets. In 1972, as part of the effort to restore the Square to its early appearance, this huge building was moved ninety feet to the south, to its current location. The Shober House (see p. 108) was subsequently reconstructed on the corner of Church and West streets.

711 Church Street
Lehman Hall 1892
Lot 16

This two-story common-bond brick building first served as a dormitory for Salem College. The original porch across the facade was removed after 1917 and replaced with the Colonial-Revival doorway with fluted columns and delicate fanlight, and paired windows on the second floor.

In the nineteenth century, the site of this building was traversed by two streets, Mink (renamed Shober) Street, and Coon (renamed Liberia, and then Blum) Street. These streets were occupied primarily by African-Americans who worked in Salem households and businesses and at the College and Academy. At one time Blum Street went toward Happy Hill, the area that became one of the first places in the South where freedmen could purchase property, from 1871.

730 Church Street
Ada Allen House c. 1939
Lot 24

This handsome house recalls many Federal characteristics of the John Vogler House on Main Street (see p. 83), including such distinguishing features as interior end chimneys, the symmetrical brick facade, a front entrance with pediment hood and "X" light transom over the door, and flat arches with keys over the windows and door. Miss Allen and her sister Annie were leaders in the initial efforts to preserve the early town of Salem.

Church Street
Mary Babcock Dormitory 1957
Lot 16

This building, Bahnson Infirmary, and Gramley Dormitory are good examples of the Moravian Revival style, incorporating such features as Flemish bond, high gable roofs with dormers, relieving arches over the windows, and Moravian hoods over the entrances.

721 Church Street
Bahnson Memorial Infirmary 1925
Lot 17
Lot 17 was traditionally used for outbuildings and gardens for the householders on Main Street.

801 Church Street
Dale E. Gramley Dormitory 1965
Lot 18
From 1804 to 1858, lots 18 and 19 were used as the garden of the Girls' Boarding School.

813–817 Church Street
Reich House and Shop 1824 and 1832, restored 1961
Lot 20
In 1823 tin- and coppersmith Christoph Reich received permission to build a frame house on Lot 20. He died during construction of the house, and his son Jacob finished the building in 1824. Together with his mother, Catherina Transou, Jacob practiced the coppersmith, tinsmith, and sheet-iron trades, first in the house, and then, after its completion in 1832, in the separate shop building. The house is similar in style to the 1822 John Leinbach House on Main Street. Sometime early in the house's history (possibly when Reich moved his business to the new shop building), the original interior end chimney on the north side was replaced with a single-shoulder stepped exterior end chimney. Several details reflect the coppersmith's trade: the metal drip above the entry, the four-light transom with pewter muntins over the door, and the metal downspout.

Jacob's son William Augustus Reich achieved fame throughout western North Carolina as a magician and showman, billing himself as "Gus Rich, the Wizzard of the Blue Ridge."

823 Church Street
Anna Johanna Vogler House 1827
Lot 95
This house was built by gunsmith Christoph Vogler, whose first house in Salem was on Main Street (see p. 100). He died shortly after moving into the house, but his widow Anna Johanna Stauber occupied the house until her death in 1870. Of all the brick houses in Salem, this one is unique in that its facade is in Flemish bond while all other walls are in common bond.

900 Church Street
House Late nineteenth century
Lot 97
This one-story frame cottage was built on the back of lot 97 in the latter half of the nineteenth century, possibly to house servants who worked in the Kuehln House on Main Street (see p. 102).

907 Church Street
House 1891–1912
Lot 95
This one-story brick cottage was built between 1891 and 1912, according to evidence from maps dating from those years. It is sited on a southern parcel of the Anna Johanna Vogler lot.

The Reich House and Shop.

909 Church Street
House 1891–1912
Lot 104
Sometime between 1891 and 1912, the original house on this location, the 1841 Fishel House, was removed and this one-and-a-half-story frame house constructed. According to legend, the house was once occupied by a ghost, an elderly lady with a cane, who would tap on the floor and open and slam doors. The ghost has been coaxed to leave, but earlier occupants of the house dealt with this problem by removing all the interior doors and storing them in the attic!

Church Street
St. Philips Complex
Strangers' Graveyard/African American Graveyard, 1772-1859, restored 2003
Log Church, 1823, reconstructed 2003
African Moravian Church (later St. Philips Church), 1861, with 1890 addition, restored 2003
Lot 104
In 1772 a separate graveyard for non-Moravians, or Strangers, was created on this lot. The first burial took place here in 1775 after the death of Michael Jordan, a visitor to Salem. By 1790 Africans and African Americans were buried in this graveyard, and by 1816, all African and African American Moravians were buried here. This practice continued until 1859 when a new graveyard was established near God's Acre.

In 1823 the Female Missionary Society sponsored the building of the log church for Africans and African Americans on this site just south of the graveyard. By 1861, just before the outbreak of the Civil War, a larger brick church was built to the east of the graveyard. A front addition to the church was built over part of the graveyard in 1890 to create more classroom space. The St. Philips congregation moved to a new church in 1952.

Work began in 1999 to restore the brick church to its 1920s exterior appearance. The sanctuary has been restored, as have the church original pews. The log church, once used as a home and as a Freedman's Hospital, was demolished early in the twentieth century, and was reconstructed in 2003.

The Lick-Boner House on Salt Street is an excellent example of an early log house in Salem.

920 Church Street
House c. 1920
Lot 99

This house is built on the rear of lot 99, on which the 1832 Lewis Eberhardt House and Shop stand (see page 102). Built after 1917, this house and the one next to it, 922 Church Street, represent the early twentieth-century trend to subdivide Salem's original lots to allow for development.

922 Church Street
Perryman House c. 1910
Lot 99

While the 1891 *Bird's Eye View of Salem* map shows a one-and-a-half-story house at this location, and 1912 and 1917 insurance maps show a house with another configuration, it is unclear what relationship the present house has to the earlier structures.

Salt Street

498 Salt Street
Denke House 1831, moved to this site 1970
Lot 75

The Denke house, originally located on Factory Row, was the home of Christian Friedrich Denke, a minister who had worked as a missionary among the Delaware Indians for many years, and his second wife, Maria Steiner (see her biography, page 63). It is an excellent example of a symmetrical, central-hall house, with interior end chimneys, that became popular in the nineteenth century. Several features reflect classicist leanings: the symmetrical facade and floor plan, and the pedimented front portico.

The Denke House is the only example of a Salem historic building moved within the district. (Other historic structures, such as the Tavern Barn and the Volz shed, have been moved from other areas into the district to replace similar structures that were destroyed). The move raised debate about the integrity of the restoration of Salem, but was justified by the value of the house as an example of its type and the fact that, in its dilapidated state, it would have been demolished at its original location.

The site was originally part of the Single Brothers' complex of orchards, gardens, and pastures for livestock. It also held the White Tannery, where deerskins were tanned for glove leather.

500 Salt Street
Christman House 1824, restored 1969
Lot 74

This house, built by carriage maker and wheelwright Jacob Christman, represents an earlier house style than its neighbor, the Denke House, which was built only eight years later. A two-story frame house, it has a plan of four rooms around a central chimney with an asymmetrical facade. It has a steep gable roof and, in the rear, a one-story shed roof extension with a porch and an enclosed room. Christman's trade is shown in the bars over the basement windows, which are made from metal wheel rims.

508 Salt Street
Salt-Flax House 1815 (?)
enlarged mid-19th C., 1879
Lot 73

Originally a one-room log building used as a storage shed by John Leinbach for his trade in salt and flax seed, this house has been altered considerably over the years. The salt trade it represented gave the street its name.

By the mid-nineteenth century, the building was functioning as a dwelling; a lean-to was added to the west side, with a kitchen in the cellar. In 1879 the house was enlarged again, with an addition on the south side and the front porch running the length of the house. The front gable and a wing at the back were added by 1907.

This is one of the few historic buildings in Salem that has not been restored to a pre-1856 state. Rather, it is an example of how architecture and building use evolve over time. A display on the front porch illustrates the changes to the building.

512 Salt Street
Lick-Boner House 1786, restored 1951–52
Lot 73

Carpenter Martin Lick built this log house in 1786, with three rooms around a central chimney and stairs leading to a loft above. It was purchased in 1795 by John Leinbach, a shoemaker who also traded in salt and flax seed, and ran an oil mill at another location. Leinbach built a half-timbered lean-to on the north side of the house for his workshop, with walls filled with wattle and daub and covered with boards. He also added a front porch (now removed) over the street and a back porch.

A few years after Leinbach's death, Thomas Jacob Boner and his wife Phoebe bought the house. They had four children, one of whom was the noted poet, John Henry Boner (1845–1902). As well as publishing several volumes of poetry, John Henry worked at the General Printing Office in Washington, D.C., and as literary editor of the *New York World*.

522 Salt Street
Hagen House 1816 and 1828, restored 1957
Lot 72

Like the Lick-Boner House next door, the Hagen House was built of logs on a one-and-a-half story plan, with stone foundation, central chimney, and asymmetrical facade. It was covered in weatherboards at an undetermined point in time.

John Hagen, a tailor who had worked as a missionary to "the Northern Indians," made several additions to the house and yard by 1828: a bake oven, a back porch over a work kitchen at the ground level, and a front porch. The house was restored to its 1828 appearance in 1957.

One of John and Maria Hagen's sons was Francis Hagen, the composer of the Christmas hymn "Morning Star."

524 Salt Street
Solomon Lick House 1822, restored 1972
Lot 71

Following the pattern of other houses on Salt Street, this house was a one-and-a-half story log house, with three rooms clustered around a central chimney. It has undergone more alterations than its neighbors; in the second half of the nineteenth century, it was raised to two stories, and in 1907 was moved away from the street. In 1972 it was moved back to its original location and restored to its original one-and-a-half story configuration. The barn was reconstructed in 1997 on the basis of archaeological investigation.

The inhabitants of Salt Street were closely linked by work and family ties. Solomon Lick was the son of Martin and Barbara Lick, who built the first house on the street in 1786. They occupied this house in 1826, when Solomon moved outside of town to the oil mill owned by John Leinbach, who was then living in the house the Licks had built.

The lot on the corner of Salt and Academy streets was the site of a sickle-smith's shop and a "grinding mill," run by the Single Brothers. After 1817, Samuel Senseman took over the site and built a house and blacksmith shop.

Across the Salem Bypass

200 Brookstown Avenue
Salem Cotton Mill 1837

In an attempt to share in the expansion of the textile industry then sweeping the South, the Moravians decided in 1836 to build a cotton mill, which was constructed in 1837. For the first time, shares in a Salem industry were sold—to several congregation officers, including the Inspector of the Girls' School, and to private individuals. The mill struggled financially in the 1840s, and finally in 1854 was bought by John Morehead, a former governor of North Carolina. The Fries family acquired the mill after the Civil War and in 1880 a large addition was made, creating the Arista Mills.

The mill that was constructed in 1837 now constitutes the western half of the mill complex on Brookstown Avenue. Its stone foundation, original east wall, and monitor roof are still intact. The complex is an excellent example of adaptive reuse of historic buildings; it now houses an inn, a restaurant, and offices.

434 Factory Row
Patterson House 1857
Lot 87

Rufus Patterson built this two-story brick Greek Revival house in 1857 with a symmetrical facade,

simple pedimented portico, and balanced external chimneys. At one time the original portico was replaced by a porch running across the front of the house. The original portico was restored around 1980.

Patterson came to Salem in 1854 to manage the Salem Cotton Mill. He became a prominent member of the Salem community, serving as chairman of the Court of Appeals and Quarter Sessions, and later as mayor of Salem. His second wife, Mary Fries, was the daughter of Lisetta Vogler and Francis Fries, the early Salem industrialist.

440 Factory Row
E. T. Ackerman House 1856
Lot 88

Edwin Ackerman, the son of John Ackerman, built this house in a Greek Revival town house style; the narrow, two-bay facades give it a row-house impression. To produce the effect of symmetry, the north chimney is false, constructed only to balance the one on the south. The ornamental brackets and railings are a later Victorian addition.

448 Factory Row
Sussdorff House 1839
Lot 89

Christian Friedrich Sussdorff originally had this house built as a one-and-a-half-story brick structure. After he sold it in 1854, the new owner added a second story; the kitchen ell was added in 1880. Sussdorff was Salem's first horticulturist, trained in Europe. Since he could not find full-time employment in his field, he took on other jobs, from piano tuning to managing the cotton mill on Brookstown Avenue.

The lot on the corner of West Street and Factory Row is the original site of the Denke House, now on Salt Street.

500 Factory Row
John Ackerman House 1822, reconstructed 1985
Lot 91

John Ackerman, a cooper, built this one-and-a-half-story log house, covered with weatherboards, on a center-chimney plan, with an asymmetrical facade. Typical of early Salem houses—but unlike the later houses on this street—it was built directly on the sidewalk.

A back view of the Inspectors' House, with the spire of Home Moravian Church in the background.

A back view of the Inspectors' House, with the spire of Home Moravian Church in the background.

512 Factory Row
Livingston Clinard House c. 1875
Lot 92

This one-and-a-half-story Victorian cottage has an abundance of charming architectural details, from the molded latticework in the front gable, to the arched pillars on the front porch, to its tall, slender windows.

The area around the intersection of Factory Row and Academy Street was the site of several important early industries in Salem. On the south side of Academy Street, near the modern Salem Bypass, there was a slaughterhouse, which was run by the Single Brothers. On the corner of Factory Row and Academy Street, the congregation-run Red Tannery was located; it produced heavier leathers for shoes and harnesses, among other things (as opposed to the White Tannery on Salt Street, which produced glove leather from deerskin). The creek that ran alongside this lot, which now emerges on the other side of Academy Street, was called Tanner's Run. On the opposite side of Academy Street was a brewery, which was also run by the congregation.

East and West Cross Streets

11 E. Academy Street
Inspectors' House 1811
with sections added in 1838 and 1850
Lot 29

In 1809 a new residence for the Inspector, or headmaster, of the Girls' School was proposed. Completed in 1811, the fine one-and-a-half story brick house has walls laid in Flemish bond with dark headers and set on a raised stuccoed basement. It has a symmetrical five-bay facade with interior end chimneys, cove and bead cornice under the roof line, and elliptical relieving arches over the windows. The centered doorway has its original arched hood, a feature unique to Salem. The ogee window tracery above the door is very similar to that on the family entrance of the Winkler Bakery.

Additions to the west of the building, made in 1838 and 1850, share many details with the original structure, such as the arches over the windows, the cornice and roof lines, and the use of end chimneys.

The original house is now used by Salem Academy and College for administrative purposes; the additions house the Salem College Bookstore.

3 East Academy Street
Boys' School 1794, restored 1954
Lot 30

An Old Salem exhibit building; see p. 67.

10 Academy Street
Single Brothers' Workshop 1771
reconstructed 1979
Lot 61

The original Single Brothers' Workshop was constructed as a story-and-a-half double-pen log building with a gable roof. The two "pens," or log sections, were connected with a half-timbered section. The workshop provided more space for trade shops; it housed a blacksmith shop, bakery, weaving room, carpenter's and joiner's shop, and locksmith's shop.

In an effort to rein in the Single Brothers' debts, the workshop was sold in 1819 to Matthew Reuz, who operated a toy shop on the premises. The building was torn down by 1921. In 1979 Old Salem reconstructed the workshop based on archaeological evidence and the original building plans. It is now used as an education center for museum programs.

The Single Brothers' Gardens, located adjacent to the Workshop, are currently under restoration. The 38,000 square feet of gardens will restore the landscape to its early-nineteenth century appearance and is one of the largest garden restoration projects in America.

Single Brothers' Workshop not open for touring.

12 West Street
Gottlieb Shober House 1785,
reconstructed 1979
Lot 28

Gottlieb Shober was one of Salem's most versatile residents. He was a tinsmith, paper mill owner, house painter, lawyer, politician, teacher, organist, and Salem's first postmaster (from 1792). In his business dealings and general behavior, he constantly challenged the church elders. In 1810, he was ordained as a Lutheran minister, a step that would have had any other Moravian banished from the town. It is a tribute to Shober's value to the community that he was allowed to continue to live in Salem.

The Shober House was destroyed in 1928 or 1929, making way for Gramley Library of Salem College to be built on the site in 1937. In 1971, in the interest of bringing Salem Square closer to its early appearance, the brick library building was moved ninety feet to the south, to its present location. The Shober House was reconstructed based on archaeological and documentary evidence, including photographs of the original house. The reconstruction used several features typical of late eighteenth-century houses in Salem: a central chimney plan, Flemish bond brickwork with dark or glazed headers, elliptical relieving arches, and a stucco foundation. It now houses the Salem College Admissions Office.

10 West Street
Traugott Bagge House 1787, reconstructed 1970
Lot 27
In 1787 Traugott Bagge requested permission to build a house on the lot opposite the Community Store for his employee, Brother Biewighausen. He was then living two blocks to the north in the Second House, which was, according to Brother Bagge, "too far away for him for his service in the store." Brother Bagge built the stone house along similar lines as the Community Store. It had stone rubble walls covered with stucco that was scored with lines to imitate the look of cut stone. The gables of this house were brick, laid in Flemish bond, whereas those of the store were shingled. The stone section of the house has a central chimney; a frame addition from 1821 has an end chimney.

The house was torn down around 1920. In 1970, it was reconstructed to its 1821 configuration, with a frame addition originally built as an apothecary. On the east side of the lot, a carriage shed added by a later owner has also been reconstucted.

8 West Street
Anna Catharina House 1771, reassembled 1954
Lot 64
This house was the first to be built in Salem with a timber frame, rather than logs or half-timbering. Built by surveyor Philip Christian Gottlieb Reuter for himself and his wife, Anna Catharina, it was originally sited on Main Street where the John Vogler house now stands. The central chimney plan had three rooms on the main floor, one of which Reuter used for working on his maps. Reuter died in 1777, and Anna Catharina lived in the house off and on until her death in 1816. In that year, John Vogler obtained permission to build on lot 64. He moved this house to the back of the lot, where it was used as an outbuilding and later as a carriage house. In 1947 the house was disassembled and stored by the Society of Colonial Dames; it was reconstructed, using the original timbers, in 1954.

Anna Catharina Antes Kalberlahn Reuter Heinzmann Ernst, one of the most intriguing early Moravian women, is the subject of a fictionalized memoir, *The Road to Salem*, by Adelaide Fries. She came to Bethabara in 1758 as the wife of the first doctor in Wachovia, Hans Martin Kalberlahn, who died the next year during a virulent fever epidemic. She would be married three times more, to Reuter from 1762 to 1777, to minister Casper Heinzmann from 1780 to 1783, and to minister Jacob Ernst from 1786 to 1802. In her own right she held responsible positions in the Moravian Church, and it may have been because of her sense of duty to the church that she agreed to her last two marriages. Her last two husbands' work took her to the towns of Friedberg and Bethabara, and she served these communities as deaconess and trusted adviser. Many years before her fourth husband died, her little house in Salem had been converted to a Widow's House, and she lived there until she died at the age of ninety.

12 Blum Street
House 1912–1917
Lot 23
By the time this house was built in the early twentieth century, Salem was a densely populated area. This narrow two-bay, gable-front house was built on a small lot carved out between the Zevely Inn, on Main Street, and a house on the corner of Blum and Church streets that has since been demolished. The back of Lot 23 once held a log shed that served as a powder magazine during the Revolutionary War.

15 Walnut Street
Siewers Cabinet Shop 1842 and 1845–50.
Lot 102
The gable-front frame portion of this house was built in 1842 as a cabinetmaker's shop by the brothers Jacob and John Siewers. John Siewers built the brick house on Main Street at the front of lot 102 in 1844; Jacob built the frame house opposite it in 1845.

This is one of the few original shops still existing in Salem, and it is unusual in that it was planned as a two-story structure. Probably around 1845 to 1850, the brick section of the house and the front porch were added. The building has functioned as a dwelling since the late nineteenth century.

The Anna Catharina House, which originally stood on Main Street, was the last home of surveyor Christian Reuter and his wife, Anna Catharina.

Planning Your Visit to Old Salem

To receive information about Old Salem by mail, call 1-888-OLD-SALEM (1-888-653-7253). For hours of operation, ticket prices, and directions to Old Salem, call 1-336-721-7300 or visit Old Salem's web site (**www.oldsalem.org**). Special rates and programs are available for groups of 14 or more with a confirmed reservation. For more information, call the Group and Tour Sales Office at 1-800-441-5305.

Look for these symbols in the guidebook and on the accompanying map to find information and services:

Ticket Required Exhibit buildings in the historic area that require a Visitor Ticket have this symbol in the Architecture Keys in the text and on the map. The "All-in-One" ticket includes admission to Old Salem, MESDA guided tours, the St. Philips Complex, The Children's Museum, and The Toy Museum. Visitors age 5 and older need a ticket (except at The Children's Museum, where visitors 4 and older need a ticket for admission). Tickets can be purchased at the Visitor Center, the Frank L. Horton Museum Center, T.Bagge: Merchant, and J. Blum: Printer and Merchant.

Information The Visitor Center, T.Bagge: Merchant, J.Blum: Printer and Merchant, and the Horton Museum Center sell tickets and provide information and services to get you started on your tour. The Visitor Center also provides other services:
- A guide to demonstrations and special events that will take place during your visit.
- A special map and routing suggestions for visitors with disabilities. The Visitor Center and the Horton Museum Center facilities (MESDA, the Gallery at Old Salem, and the Children's Museum) are fully wheelchair-accessible, as are some, but not all, of the exhibit buildings in Old Salem.
- Brochures translated into French, German, Italian, Japanese, and Spanish.
- A Lost-and-Found section.
- A display tracing the history of the Moravians.
- Slide shows dramatizing life in Salem in the eighteenth century, orienting visitors to the museum town as it is today.

First Aid supplies are available at the Visitor Center and at all Old Salem exhibit buildings.

Dining Please call for hours and menu information.
- The Old Salem Corner Deli, in the Visitor Center, serves sandwiches on fresh bread from our Winkler Bakery, salads, beverages, seasonal soups or ice cream, as well as world-famous Krispy Kreme original glazed doughnuts and coffee. 900 Old Salem Road. 336-499-7953.
- The Salem Tavern, in the 1816 Tavern annex, serves lunch and dinner in a setting evoking nineteenth-century Salem. Dinner reservations are recommended. 736 S. Main Street. 336-748-8585.
- The Village Soda Shop, upstairs over Winkler Bakery, serves sandwiches, ice cream, and beverages. 527 S. Main Street. 336-748-1498.

Restrooms are located in the Visitor Center, Horton Museum Center, Single Brothers' Gardens (at West Street), Tavern Woodshed, and in the Vierling Barn.

Parking is available at the Visitor Center on Old Salem Road. When these lots are filled, look for signs directing you to overflow parking. Please respect posted speed limits, one-way streets, and parking signs.

Vending machines serving soft drinks are found on the lower level of T. Bagge: Merchant and in the Tavern Woodshed. Picnic tables are located along Salt Street to the north of the Visitor Center as well as under the walkway at the Horton Museum Center.

Shopping Old Salem has a variety of shops that have specialty gifts, books, and souvenirs. Friends of Old Salem and Friends of MESDA and the Collections receive a discount of 10 percent on purchases in Old Salem-run shops.

- The Market-place. Located in the Visitor Center, this shop offers unique and unusual items relating to Old Salem. 900 Old Salem Road. 336-499-7954.
- The Old Salem Souvenir Shop. Logo apparel, souvenirs, and local and regional gifts and books are available in this shop located in the Visitor Center. 900 Old Salem Road. 336-499-7950.
- T. Bagge: Merchant. Located in Salem's original Community Store, T. Bagge offers traditional Moravian and Old Salem gift items. 626 S. Main Street. 336-721-7389.
- J. Blum: Printer and Merchant. In the house and shop of Salem's first printer, the Blum Shop sells books, stationery, writing implements, and other gift items. 724 S. Main Street. 336-721-7325.
- The MESDA Bookstore has an extensive collections of books on decorative arts and southern history and culture. 924 S. Main Street. (in the Horton Museum Center). 336-721-7369.
- The Toy Shop, in the Horton Museum Center, offers merchandise and reproductions relating to the Toy Museum as well as products based on objects in the MESDA and Old Salem collections. 924 S. Main Street. 336-779-6140.
- Winkler Bakery bakes bread and Moravian sugar cake in an authentic wood-fired oven. The bakery also sells cakes, jams, traditional Moravian cookies, and mixes for many baked goods and other favorite tastes from the past. 527 S. Main Street. 336-721-7302.
- The Old Salem Catalog offers Moravian cookies and Old Salem gift items. To receive a catalog or place an order, call 1-800-822-5151 or visit our Website at *www.oldsalem.org*.
- Moravian Book and Gift Shop features books and gift items. All proceeds support Moravian Church outreach ministries. 614 S. Main Street. 336-723-6262.

Overnight Accommodations

- The Augustus Zevely Inn, with bed-and-breakfast accommodations in the tradition of its original owner, Dr. Zevely, who took in overnight guests when the Tavern was full. 803 S. Main Street. 336-748-9299.
- The Brookstown Inn, in the former Salem Cotton Mill. 200 Brookstown Avenue. 336-725-1120.
- The Best Western Salem Inn & Suites. 127 S. Cherry Street. 336-725-8561.
- The Hawthorne Inn & Conference Center. 420 High Street. 336-777-3000.
- The Wingate Inn. 125 S. Main Street. 336-714-2800.
- The Henry F. Shaffner House Bed & Breakfast Inn. 150 S. Marshall Street. 336-777-0052.

Become a member!

Enjoy special members' benefits when you join the Friends of Old Salem or the Friends of MESDA and the Collections and support research and restoration efforts. Depending on which program and/or level you choose, you may also receive admissio n benefits for one or more individuals. You will also receive advance notice and discounts for special events, and a 10% discount in all Old Salem shops. Join when you visit to take advantage of your special benefits, or call 336-721-7328 or visit **www.oldsalem.org** for more information.

Glossary

Aeltesten Conferenz (Elders' Conference) The board in charge of the spiritual affairs of the congregation.

Aufseher Collegium (Board of Supervisors) The board in charge of the material and financial affairs of the congregational community.

Bohemia The former kingdom in Europe, now part of the Czech Republic, where the Unitas Fratrum originated among the followers of John Huss.

Brother The term used by the Moravians to refer to a man in the congregation.

Choir system The organization of the congregation according to age, gender, and marital status: Single Sisters, Single Brothers, MarriedSisters, Married Brothers, Widows, Widowers, Older Boys, Older Girls, Little Boys, and Little Girls. Each choir had its own festival days, and administration; in addition, the Single Brothers and Single Sisters choirs ran their own business enterprises, which were managed by the choir's diaconie (see below).

Common bond Brickwork in which the bricks are laid so that only stretchers (long side of bricks) are exposed.

Congregation town A town where nearly every aspect of life was governed by the Moravian Church. The church owned all land in the town, decided what trades would be represented, and controlled civil as well as spiritual affairs. It also had a say in personal matters, such as the training an individual could receive and whom he or she could marry. Only members of the Moravian Church could live in the congregation town, and a member who did not abide by the church's rules and guidelines would be asked to leave the community.

Deaconess A woman, often the wife of a deacon, a minister, or a bishop, who assisted with the spiritual work among the Sisters in the congregation.

Diaconie The business organization of a congregation or a choir.

Diary A daily record, or diary, of events in a Moravian town, kept by that town's minister. It included information about important church decisions, community celebrations, marriages, an individual's choice of a trade, and details about such practical matters as crops and the weather.

Elders' Conference See Aeltesten Conferenz.

Elliptical arch An arch composed of part of an ellipse, used over doors and windows to distribute the weight of the walls above them.

Fachwerk (Also called half-timbering) A building method brought from Europe by Moravian builders in which spaces in timber-framed walls are filled in with brick or wattle-and-daub (a filling material made of sticks woven into panels and covered with mud mixed with straw or hair).

Flemish bond Brickwork in which headers (ends of bricks) alternate with stretchers (long sides of bricks) on each row, with the headers centered on the stretchers on the rows above and below.

Fremde See Stranger.

Gemein Haus The Congregation House in early Moravian communities, containing a meeting hall for worship (the Saal) and living quarters for ministers, their families, and other members of the congregation.

God's Acre The burial ground in a Moravian settlement. Honoring the concept of "democracy in death," it is divided into sections representing the choir system. Single Sisters, Single Brothers, Married Sisters, Married Brothers, and children are buried in sections dedicated to their choirs. Each grave is marked with a simple flat stone.

Half-timbering See Fachwerk.

Helfer (Helper) The leading minister of the congregation, or the leader of a Choir. More often the term Pfleger (see below) is used.

Helfer Conferenz (Helpers' Conference) An advisory board made up of ministers. Later known as the Provincial Helpers, Conference, and, after that, as the Provincial Elders Conference. It became the chief administrative body of the Moravian Church, Southern Province.

Herrnhut The settlement founded by Count Zinzendorf as a refuge for members of the Unitas Fratrum; its name means "the Lord's watch," or "the Lord's protection." From this town the Moravian Church spread throughout the world.

Hussites Early followers of John Huss, most of whom lived in Moravia and Bohemia.

Inspector The head of the Girls' School or the Boys' School.

Kick eave An eave created at the outer edge of a roof that otherwise would stop on the wall supports, by placing a wedge of wood between the roofing material and the rafters. The extension of the roof shunted rainwater away from the building, protecting the walls from water damage.

Lebenslauf (Life story) The spiritual biography or autobiography recorded at the death of each member of the Moravian congregation. It would be read at his or her funeral and filed in the church archives. Also called a memoir.

Locking plate A horizontal wooden beam, part of the roof construction, that is set into the wall of a brick building at the base of the roof. It secures, or locks, the roof to the walls.

Lot A religious ritual used by the early Moravians and other religious groups to determine God's will in making important or difficult decisions. The practice was inspired by biblical rituals described in Numbers 33:54 and in Acts 1:26. Rolled pieces of paper with key words printed on them were placed in a bowl and one was picked out. If the slip read "yes" or "no," a decision was accepted. If the slip drawn was blank, that indicated that the decision required more consideration.

Lovefeast A religious fellowship service, accompanied by singing, during which the congregation shares a simple meal, usually of specially prepared bread and coffee or tea. The Lovefeast is said to date from the birthday of the Renewed Moravian Church in Herrnhut on August 13, 1727. It was held to celebrate special occasions. The practice is based on the Agape, or common meal, of the early Christians.

Memoir See Lebenslauf.

Moravia A province in Europe, now part of the Czech Republic, where many members of the Unitas Fratrum settled. After they were driven into exile, the name Moravian was often used to describe the Unitas Fratrum.

Moravians Members of the church officially called the Unitas Fratrum.

Moravian Church The church officially called the Unitas Fratrum, or Unity of the Brethren. See Unitas Fratrum.

Oeconomie The system of common housekeeping and community cooperation that undergirded early Moravian communities, including Bethabara.

Oeconomus The chief financial and business officer of such Moravian settlements as Salem.

Pfleger Literally, the one who cares for others. A name used to describe the pastor of the congregation, or the leader of a Choir. A woman would be called Pflegerin. Also called Helfer or Helferin.

Saal A hall or sanctuary in which religious services take place, whether in the church, the Gemein Haus, or a choir house.

Saal diener A man who served as a sexton or usher in church services, considered a position of great responsibility. A woman who served in this capacity was called a Saal dienerin.

Singstunde A church service devoted to singing rather than preaching.

Sister The term used by the Moravians to refer to a woman in the congregation.

Stranger (in German, Fremde) The term used for someone who was not connected to the Moravian Church. While the Moravians welcomed Strangers as visitors to Salem, they kept them—and their worldly ways—at a distance.

Timber framing A building method that uses large, squared wood members, typically joined using pegged mortise-and-tenon construction to connect the pieces together.

Unitas Fratrum (Unity of the Brethren) The first religious group to break away from the Catholic Church, in 1457. A Protestant faith similar in many ways to Lutheranism. It has more than 800,000 believers around the world, with around 50,000 in the United States. Its headquarters are in Herrnhut, Germany. Among English-speaking peoples it is widely referred to as the Moravian Church.

Vorsteher The business manager and treasurer of the congregation or one of the choirs.

Wachovia (Wachau) The name given to the nearly 100,000-acre tract of land that the Moravians purchased in piedmont North Carolina in 1753. It was named after the region in Austria where the ancestral estate of Count Nicholas von Zinzendorf was located.

Weatherboard Exterior sheathing for a frame building generally composed of sawn, horizontally lapped boards. Also called clapboard.

Further reading

Albright, Frank P.
Johann Ludwig Eberhardt and His Salem Clocks.
Chapel Hill, N.C.:
University of North Carolina Press, 1978.

Bivins, John, Jr.
The Moravian Potters in North Carolina.
Chapel Hill, N.C.:
University of North Carolina Press, 1972.

Bivins, John, Jr., and Paula Welshimer.
Moravian Decorative Arts in North Carolina: An Introduction to the Old Salem Collection. Winston-Salem, N.C.:
Old Salem, Inc., 1981.

Bivins, John, Jr., and Forsyth Alexander.
Regional Arts of the Early South: A Sampling from the Collection of the Museum of Early Southern Decorative Arts.
Winston-Salem, N.C.:
MESDA, 1991.

Chapman, Sarah Bahnson.
Bright and Gloomy Days: The Civil War Correspondence of CaptainCharles Frederic Bahnson, a Moravian Confederate.
Knoxville: University of Tennessee Press, 2003.

Comenius, John Amos.
The School of Infancy.
Chapel Hill, N.C.:
University of North Carolina Press, 1956.

Crews, C. Daniel.
My Name Shall Be There: The Founding of Salem (with Friedberg, Friedland).
Winston-Salem, N.C.:
Moravian Archives, 1995.

_____.
Neither Slave Nor Free: Moravians, Slavery, and a Church That Endures.
Winston-Salem, N.C.:
Moravian Archives, 1998.

_____.
A Storm in the Land: Southern Moravians and the Civil War.
Winston-Salem, N.C.:
Moravian Archives, 1997.

_____.
Through Fiery Trials: The Revolutionary War and the Moravians.
Winston-Salem, N.C.:
Moravian Archives, 1996.

_____.
Villages of the Lord: The Moravians come to North Carolina.
Winston-Salem, N.C.:
Moravian Archives, 1995.

Crews, C. Daniel, and Lisa D. Bailey.
Records of the Moravians in North Carolina, Vol. XII, 1856-1866.
Raleigh: Division of Archives and History, North Carolina Department of Cultural Resources, 2000.

Comenius, John Amos.
The School of Infancy.
Chapel Hill, N.C.:
University of North Carolina Press, 1956.

Fries, Adelaide L.
The Road to Salem.
Winston-Salem, N.C.:
John F. Blair, Publisher, 1993.

Fries, Adelaide L., Douglas L. Rights, Minnie J. Smith, Kenneth G. Hamilton, eds.,
Records of the Moravians in North Carolina, 1752–1879.
11 volumes.
Raleigh, N.C.:
Department of Archives and History, 1922–1969.

Griffin, Frances.
Less Time for Meddling: A History of Salem Academy and College, 1772–1866.
Winston-Salem, N.C.:
John F. Blair, Publisher, 1979.

_____.
*Old Salem: An Adventure in
Historic Preservation,*
revised edition.
Winston-Salem, N.C.:
Old Salem, Inc., 1985.

Hamilton, Kenneth G. and
J. Taylor Hamilton.
*History of the Moravian Church:
The Renewed Unitas Fratrum,
1722–1957.*
Bethlehem, Penn.:
Interprovincial Board of Education,
Moravian Church
in America, 1967.

James, Hunter.
*The Quiet People of the
Land: A Story of the North Carolina
Moravians in Revolutionary Times.*
Chapel Hill, N.C.:
University of North Carolina Press,
1976.

*Journal of Early Southern
Decorative Arts,* vols. 1–29.
Articles and reviews on
southern decorative arts,
published by MESDA since 1975.

Locklair, Paula W.
*Quilts, Coverlets, and
Counterpanes: Bedcoverings from
the MESDA
and Old Salem Collections.*
Winston-Salem, N.C.:
Old Salem, Inc., 1997.

Niven, Penelope.
*Frank C. Horton and the Roads to
MESDA,* published in
*Journal of Early Southern
Decorative Arts,* Vol. XXVII, No. 1
(Summer 2001).

Rauschenberg, Bradford L.
*The Wachovia Historical Society,
1895–1995.*
Winston-Salem, N.C.:
Wachovia Historical Society, 1995.

Sensbach, Jon F.
African-Americans in Salem.
Winston-Salem, N.C.:
Old Salem, Inc., 1991.

_____.
*A Separate Canaan:
The Making of an Afro-
Moravian World in North Carolina,
1763–1840.*
Chapel Hill, N.C.:
University of North Carolina Press,
1998.

Shirley, Michael.
*From Congregation Town to Industrial
City: Culture and Social Change in a
Southern Community.*
New York:
New York University Press, 1994.

Spencer, Darrell.
*The Gardens of Salem:
The Landscape History of a Moravian
Town in North Carolina.*
Winston-Salem, N.C.:
Old Salem, Inc., 1997.

Street, Julia.
Candle Lovefeast.
Winston-Salem, N.C.:
Old Salem, Inc., 1991.

Thorp, Daniel B.
*The Moravian Community in North
Carolina: Pluralism on
the Southern Frontier.*
Knoxville, Tenn.:
University of Tennessee Press, 1989.

*A Thousand Years of Czech Culture:
Riches from the National Museum
in Prague.*
Winston-Salem, N.C.:
Old Salem, Inc., 1996.

Three Forks of Muddy Creek,
vols. 1–14.
Articles on Salem history
published by Old Salem
from 1974 to 1990.

Wachovia Historical Society, *Salem's
Remembrancers.*
Winston-Salem, N.C.:
Wachovia Historical Society, 1976.

Index

Index

Index

Credits

In the preparation of this book, many people generously shared their knowledge and expertise, their time and resources, their editorial advice and critical comments, and their skilled and sensitive understanding of Old Salem's people, history, and heritage. We are deeply grateful to each and every one, especially to the staff of Old Salem and MESDA, and the staff of the Archives of the Moravian Church in North America, Southern Province. We also appreciate the groundbreaking work of the historians and scholars who have produced valuable books and articles about the Moravian legacy.

The following institutions graciously allowed us to reproduce objects and photographs in their collections: Archives of the Moravian Church, Herrnhut, Germany; Archives of the Moravian Church in North America, Northern Province, Bethlehem, Penn.; Archives of the Moravian Church in North America, Southern Province, Winston-Salem, N.C.; Moravian Historical Society, Nazareth, Penn.; National Museum and Library, Prague, Czech Republic; Salem Academy and College Archives, Winston-Salem, N.C.; Tannenberg Historical Park, Greensboro, N.C.; Wachovia Historical Society, Winston-Salem, N.C. These institutions or the photographers are credited to the right.

Photo Credits

Photographs are identified by position as left (l.) or right (r.) and by Roman numeral (i, ii, iii, etc.) from the top.

Front cover, Daniel Welfare, *View of Salem*, lithograph, 1824, Old Salem (OS); back cover, Virginia R. Weiler (VRW); p. 2, VRW; p. 3, OS; 0p. 6, i National Museum Prague, ii, iii OS, iv Tannenbaum Historical Park, v VRW; p. 7, i, VRW, ii, iii, OS; iv, VRW; p. 8, National Museum Prague; p. 9, National Library Prague; pp. 10, 11, OS; p. 12, l. Wood Ronsaville Harlin, r. OS; p. 13, Moravian Archives Herrnhut; pp. 14, OS; 15, i, OS, ii, Moravian Archives WS; pp. 16, 17 l., Moravian Archives Herrnhut; pp. 17 r., 18, Moravian Archives WS; p. 19, VRW; p. 20, Moravian Archives WS; p. 21, OS; p. 22, Moravian Archives Bethlehem; p. 23, OS; pp. 24, 25, Moravian Archives Herrnhut; p. 26, i, private collection, ii, VRW; p. 27 (both) VRW; p. 28, i, VRW, ii, private collection; p. 29 (both) OS, ii, OS; p. 30, OS; p. 31, Moravian Archives Herrnhut; pp. 32, 33, VRW; pp. 34–35, Wood Ronsaville Harlin; p. 36 (both) OS; p. 37 (all), OS; p. 38, l. i, ii, iii, iv, OS, r. Moravian Archives WS; p. 39 (all), OS; p. 40 (all) OS; p. 41, i, Moravian Archives Herrnhut, ii, iv, OS, iii, VRW; p. 42, VRW; p. 43, i, OS, ii, iii, iv, VRW; p. 44 (both) OS; p. 45, i, ii, iii, iv, VRW; p. 46, OS; p. 47 (both) Tannenberg Historical Park; p. 48 (both), OS; p. 49, i, Jim Stanley for Old Salem, ii, OS; p. 50, i, VRW, ii, OS; p. 51, i, OS, ii, Moravian Archives Herrnhut, iii, VRW, iv, OS; p. 53, i, OS, ii, Moravian Historical Society, Nazareth; p. 54 i, Wachovia Historical Society, ii, VRW; p. 55 l., VRW, r. i, OS, ii, VRW; p. 56, VRW; p. 57 i, VRW, ii, iii, OS; pp. 58–59, Wood Ronsaville Harlin; pp. 60 i, OS, ii, OS; p. 61 i, OS, ii, iii, VRW; pp. 62, 63 i, VRW; p. 63 ii, Black Horse Studio; p. 64 (both), OS; p. 65 (all) OS; p. 66 i, OS, ii, *The Orbis Pictus of John Amos Comenius* (Syracuse, N.Y., 1887), 4; p. 67 i, VRW, ii, iii, iv, OS; p. 68 i, VRW, ii, OS; pp. 69 (all), p. 70, OS; p. 71 i, VRW, ii, OS; p. 72 i, Moravian Archives Herrnhut, ii, OS; p. 73 i, OS, ii, Archives, Salem Academy and College; p. 74 (both) OS; pp. 75 (all), 76 (both), VRW; pp. 77 (both), VRW; pp. 78, 79, OS; p. 80, i, VRW, ii, iii, OS; p. 81(all), 82 (both) OS; p. 83 i, ii, iii, OS, iv, VRW; p. 84 i, VRW, ii, OS; p. 85 i, ii, VRW, iii, OS; pp. 86, 87, OS; pp. 88, 89, OS; p. 90 i, OS, ii, VRW; pp. 91, 92, 93, 94, 95, 96, OS; p. 97, l. OS, r. i, ii, iii, OS; pp. 99, 100, 101, 102, VRW; pp. 103, 104, 105, OS; p. 106, Moravian Archives, Herrnhut; pp. 107, 108, VRW; p. 109, OS; pp. 110, 111, VRW.

Edited by Cornelia B. Wright

Revised edition edited by Gary J. Albert, director of publications, Old Salem Inc.

Design, color separation, and typesetting by Richard Sheaff, Scottsdale, Arizona

Photography for Old Salem by Wes Stewart

Map and graphics by Wood Ronsaville Harlin, Annapolis, Maryland

Printed by HarperPrints, Henderson, North Carolina

Printed in the United States of America

Library of Congress Cataloging-in-Publication Data

Niven, Penelope.
    Old Salem : the official guidebook / Penelope Niven, text; Cornelia B. Wright, street guide.—new ed.
        p. cm.
    Includes bibliographical references and index.
    ISBN 1-879704-07-2 (pbk.)
        1. Salem (N.C.)—Guidebooks. 2. Salem (N.C.)—Buildings, structures, etc.—Guidebooks.
    3. Historic buildings—North Carolina—Salem—Guidebooks. 4. Architecture—North Carolina—Salem—Guidebooks. I. Wright, Cornelia B. II. Title.

F264.S32 N58 1999
917.56'67—dc21
                        99-039890

Penelope Niven is the author of *Carl Sandburg: A Biography*; co-author, with James Earl Jones, of *Voices and Silence*; and author of *Steichen: A Biography; Carl Sandburg: Adventures of a Poet*; and *Swimming Lessons*, a memoir. She has been awarded three fellowships from the National Endowment for the Humanities and two honorary doctorates, and is Writer-in-Residence at Salem College in Winston-Salem, North Carolina.

Cornelia Wright is an author and editor living in Winston-Salem, North Carolina, and formerly Editor of Publications for Old Salem Inc.